CHICAGO'S ART DECO SKYSCRAPERS

CHICAGO'S
ART DECO
SKYSCRAPERS

Joseph Gustaitis

THE UNIVERSITY OF CHICAGO PRESS
CHICAGO AND LONDON

Unless otherwise indicated in captions, photographs by Ian McClellan.

The University of Chicago Press, Chicago 60637
The University of Chicago Press, Ltd., London

Published 2026
Printed in Canada

35 34 33 32 31 30 29 28 27 26   1 2 3 4 5

ISBN-13: 978-0-226-85052-8 (cloth)
ISBN-13: 978-0-226-85053-5 (ebook)
DOI: https://doi.org/10.7208/chicago/9780226850535.001.0001

Library of Congress Cataloging-in-Publication Data

Names: Gustaitis, Joseph, 1944– author
Title: Chicago's art deco skyscrapers / Joseph Gustaitis.
Description: Chicago : The University of Chicago Press, 2026. | Includes bibliographical references and index.
Identifiers: LCCN 2026006568 | ISBN 9780226850528 cloth | ISBN 9780226850535 ebook
Subjects: LCSH: Skyscrapers—Illinois—Chicago | Art deco (Architecture)—Illinois—Chicago | Chicago (Ill.)—Buildings, structures, etc.
Classification: LCC NA735.C4 G87 2026
LC record available at https://lccn.loc.gov/2026006568

♾ This paper meets the requirements of ANSI/NISO Z39.48-1992 (Permanence of Paper).

Authorized Representative for EU General Product Safety Regulation (GPSR) queries:
Easy Access System Europe—Mustamäe tee 50, 10621 Tallinn, Estonia,
gpsr.requests@easproject.com
Any other queries: https://press.uchicago.edu/press/contact.html

DEDICATED WITH LOVE AND THANKFULNESS TO CATHERINE, MY WIFE, PARTNER, COLLABORATOR, BIGGEST SUPPORTER, AND BEST FRIEND

Rivet-guns thundering in an iron-chested roar,
Punching white-hot clinchers on the forty-seventh floor;
Cable-hoists and air lines are stitching boiler plate;
Some one wants a fifty-decker—and they want it while
they wait.

So.

Let's climb—climb—climb!
Up to where the whistles chime,
Begging for the men they need,
Roaring at each mighty deed,
There's work to do. Let's GO!

. . . .

So.

Let's rush—rush—rush!
Where the whistles never hush,
Shrieking shrill their frantic plea,
Shouting loud for you and me,
Booming "Builders! Can't you see
There's work to do?" Let's GO!

C. S. CHAMBERLAIN, "WHISTLES"

CONTENTS

INTRODUCTION 1

NO. 1	333 NORTH MICHIGAN	17
NO. 2	CHICAGO MOTOR CLUB	27
NO. 3	10 WEST ELM	33
NO. 4	NORTHWEST TOWER	39
NO. 5	POWHATAN APARTMENTS	45
NO. 6	CARBIDE AND CARBON BUILDING	53
NO. 7	PALMOLIVE BUILDING	59
NO. 8	CHICAGO DAILY NEWS BUILDING	67
NO. 9	CIVIC OPERA HOUSE	77
NO. 10	FOREMAN STATE NATIONAL BANK	87
NO. 11	BUCKINGHAM BUILDING	95
NO. 12	LA SALLE-WACKER BUILDING	101
NO. 13	TRUSTEES SYSTEM SERVICE BUILDING	107
NO. 14	ONE NORTH LA SALLE	115
NO. 15	CHICAGO BOARD OF TRADE BUILDING	123
NO. 16	MUNDELEIN CENTER	135
NO. 17	MERCHANDISE MART	143
NO. 18	LAWSON HOUSE YMCA	153
NO. 19	CENTRAL POST OFFICE	159
NO. 20	FIELD BUILDING	167

CONCLUSION 173

ACKNOWLEDGMENTS 181

NOTES 183

INDEX 197

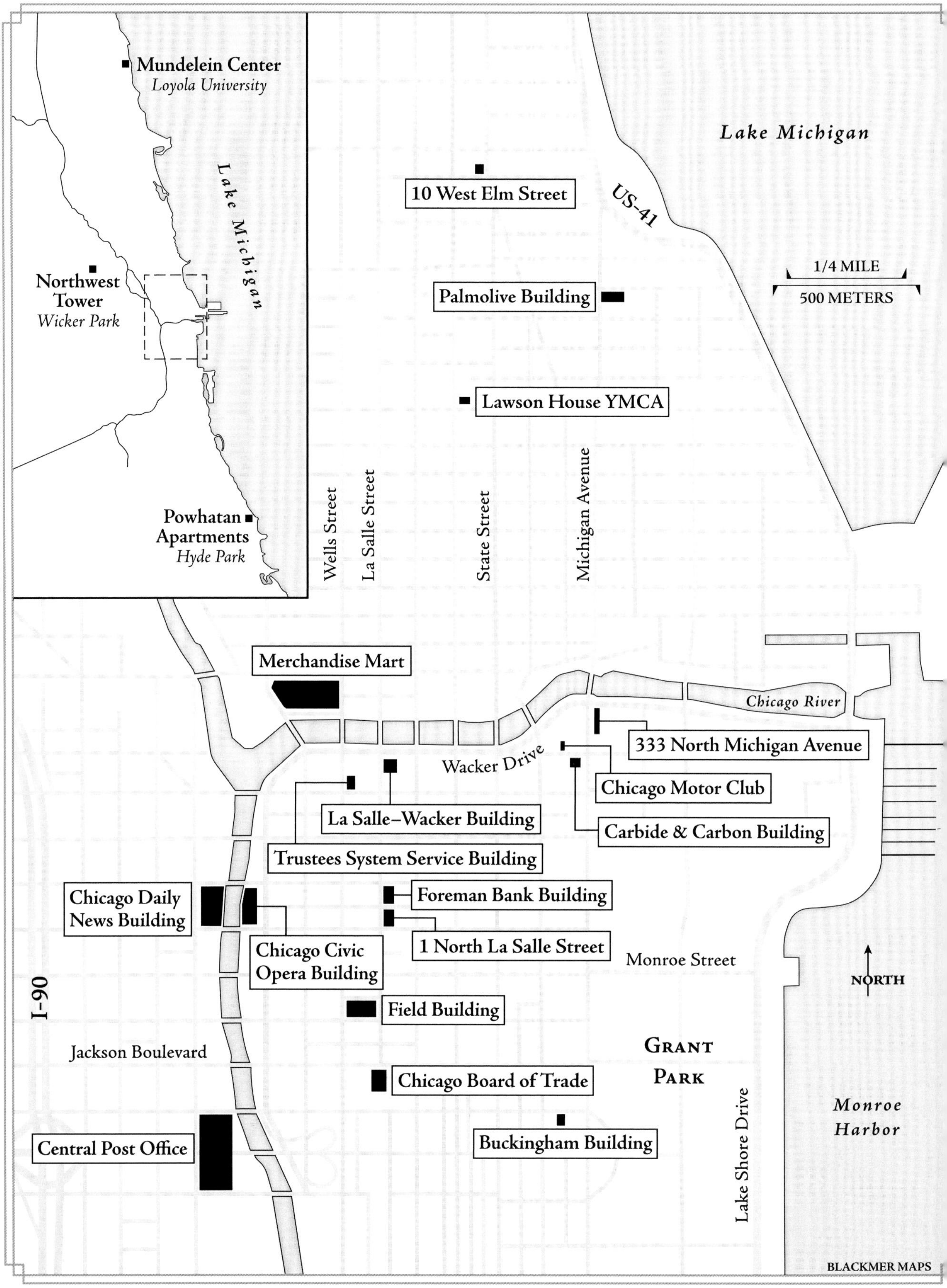

Mundelein Center
Loyola University
Lake Michigan
Northwest Tower
Wicker Park
Powhatan Apartments
Hyde Park
Lake Michigan
10 West Elm Street
US-41
1/4 MILE
500 METERS
Palmolive Building
Lawson House YMCA
Wells Street
La Salle Street
State Street
Michigan Avenue
Merchandise Mart
Chicago River
333 North Michigan Avenue
Wacker Drive
Chicago Motor Club
La Salle–Wacker Building
Carbide & Carbon Building
Trustees System Service Building
Chicago Daily News Building
Foreman Bank Building
Chicago Civic Opera Building
1 North La Salle Street
Monroe Street
NORTH
I-90
Field Building
Jackson Boulevard
Grant Park
Chicago Board of Trade
Monroe Harbor
Central Post Office
Buckingham Building
Lake Shore Drive
BLACKMER MAPS

INTRODUCTION

Soaring, self-assured, sophisticated, stylish, and raised by visionaries who foresaw a streamlined future that would unite technology and art, Chicago's Art Deco towers stand as symbols of a metropolis at the peak of its prestige, as well as of the buoyant spirit of an entire era.

People who spend any time in Chicago's downtown are familiar with some of the towers in this book. No one can miss the Merchandise Mart, the Palmolive Building, or the Chicago Board of Trade Building, and the opera house is well attended. But the results of a poll of favorite Chicago skyscrapers would probably lead with the Wrigley Building, Tribune Tower, Willis (formerly Sears) Tower, 875 North Michigan Avenue (which everyone still calls the John Hancock Center), and the Aqua, none of which are Art Deco. Yet the Art Deco skyscrapers represent more than just the modern architecture of their time; they embody a style and a viewpoint that still has much to offer. Art Deco has been called "the last of the total styles"—the term could be, and was, applied to almost anything from toasters to giant ocean liners.

Art Deco was a modern design aesthetic that arose

in the second decade of the twentieth century, flourished throughout the 1920s, and persisted in one form or another until the Second World War. Characteristics of the style include geometric patterns; lightning bolts; chevrons; sunbursts; overlapping arches; Aztec, African, and Egyptian motifs; abstracted animals; and stylized flower bouquets. Zigzag motifs were so prevalent that some historians have referred to the initial state of Art Deco as "Zig-Zag Moderne." The style, if not the name, is familiar to almost everyone. Its distinctive motifs, according to architectural photographer Carla Breeze, make Art Deco "one of the few styles of architecture that the majority of Americans can easily identify."[1] At the time, however, the term "Art Deco" wasn't used. In the 1920s some ways to describe objects in the new style were "modernistic," "streamline," "jazz moderne," "zigzag style," and "ship style," although other names were proposed. The most used term, however, was "moderne," an acknowledgment that the main impetus came from France.

Even without using the term "Art Deco," the public at the time was aware that something stylistically important was happening, especially in architecture. In 1929 one observer wrote, "One of the great features of Chicago's skyscraper development of the last decade has been the enormous improvement in the appearance of the new buildings. Order, harmony and beauty have been welded to mass and power. Splendid lines and pleasing proportions are striking characteristics of the new order." The author went on to say that this "new order" was bringing "the development of a modern American style of architecture; an architecture typifying the civilization that made it possible and embodying it in its frankness and originality the spirit of the metropolis from which it sprang."[2] This was something new. American culture and design had long taken their cues from the great cultural capitals of Europe—whether Paris, Vienna, or Amsterdam—but that was no longer necessary.

Not only were great buildings erected, but a mental shift occurred. The spirit of the era was optimistic, technological, forward-looking. With the Great War in the past and the Great Depression still in the future, the 1920s embraced industrial modernity and the scale of its booming cities. Today we esteem Chicago's Art Deco skyscrapers for their beauty and creativity, but at the time they were admired principally because (1) they rejected past aesthetics, (2) they were modern, and (3) they were American.

ORIGIN OF THE TERM "ART DECO"

Interestingly, John W. Root of the architectural firm Holabird & Root, which designed several of Chicago's Art Deco skyscrapers, didn't like the terms "moderne" or "modernistic." "The first," a commentator wrote, "he associates with some sort of atrocity, while the latter signifies to him that a designer has been tricky and done something new and different."[3]

The term "Art Deco" derives from the name of a groundbreaking 1925 exhibit held in Paris, the Exposition Internationale des Arts Décoratifs et Industriels Modernes ("Arts Décoratifs" gave way to "Art Deco"). The expo had originally been planned for 1916 but was postponed because of World War I. Architectural historians tend to say the first Art Deco building was August Perret's Theatre des Champs-Elysees in Paris, which was completed in 1913, although Belgians assert the primacy of the Palais Stoclet in Brussels (1905–1911). The first use of the term "Art Deco" was apparently by the modernist gadfly architect Le Corbusier, who published his manifesto *L'art décoratif d'aujourdhui* in the same year as the exposition. A purist who preferred minimalism, he disliked the new style for its use of ornamentation. "Modern decorative art," he said paradoxically, "is not decorated."[4] He was echoing the famous 1910 pronouncement by Austrian architect Adolf Loos, who said "Ornament is a crime," and the German design think tank known as the Bauhaus was on board with this minimalist viewpoint. Chicago designers, several of whom were educated in Paris and read the avant-garde manifestos, were aware that the outlook of the European modernists was anti-ornament, but they resisted the trend. As John Augur Holabird Jr. explained, "There was a feeling at that time if you left the building completely unadorned—well, no one could face that. You did that for warehouses, but not for downtown buildings."[5] In any case, the term Art Deco didn't catch on then.

Some historians consider the Palais Stoclet in Brussels of 1905–1911, with its modernistic tower, the first Art Deco building. Photo by PtrQs, https://commons.wikimedia.org/wiki/File:20120923_Brussels_PalaisStoclet_Hoffmann_DSC06725_PtrQs.jpg, CC BY-SA 4.0, https://creativecommons.org/licenses/by-sa/4.0/deed.en.

"Art Deco" did not become an affirmative phrase and standard art-historical term until the 1960s. Typical histories of Art Deco point to the publication in 1968 of *Art Deco of the 20s and 30s* by British art historian Bevis Hillier as the event that launched the term, but two years before Hillier's book was published, the Musée des Art Décoratifs in Paris staged the exhibition *Les Années "25": Art Déco/Bauhaus/Stijl/Esprit Nouveau.* This was one of the first uses of "Art Deco" in a curatorial context and its affiliation with three other critically approved early twentieth-century styles gave it status. Hillier himself commented that the *Années "25"* show marked the occasion when "the Art Deco revival really began to take a hold on fashion, stage-sets, book jacket design and posters." He said it had inspired him to choose, from many possibilities, the term "Art Deco" for his book—though he did also say that "Art Deco is already a name in reasonably common use." As examples, he cited a 1966 article by Hilary Gelson in *The Times* of London and one in the French magazine *Elle* a year later.[6]

In 1971, Hillier further promoted the use of the term by curating an exhibition at the Minneapolis Institute of Art called *The World of Art Deco.* In reviewing that show, Marvin D. Schwartz of *The New York Times* wrote, "Art Deco is an expression of strength in a moment of confusion and should not be overlooked," and throughout the 1970s the paper featured regular stories on the Art Deco revival.[7] Evelyn Livingstone, fashion editor for the *Chicago Tribune*, appears to have been an early adopter of the label, writing in February 1969 about contemporary artists' "fascination" with Art Deco and continuing to use the term in subsequent writings.[8] Hillier might not have coined "Art Deco," but he certainly popularized it.

By the 1960s, the conditions for a reevaluation of Art Deco were in place. Consumers of art were becoming bored with modernism's stripped-down look, and architects began promoting "postmodernism," which allowed greater latitude in historical references and decoration. Also, the destruction of classic buildings in many cities (the Chicago Stock Exchange was a particularly tragic example) gave rise to vigorous architectural preservation movements. Meanwhile, collectors were finding that easily recognizable Art Deco objects were available in flea markets and antique shops at affordable prices, while nostalgia for the Jazz Age

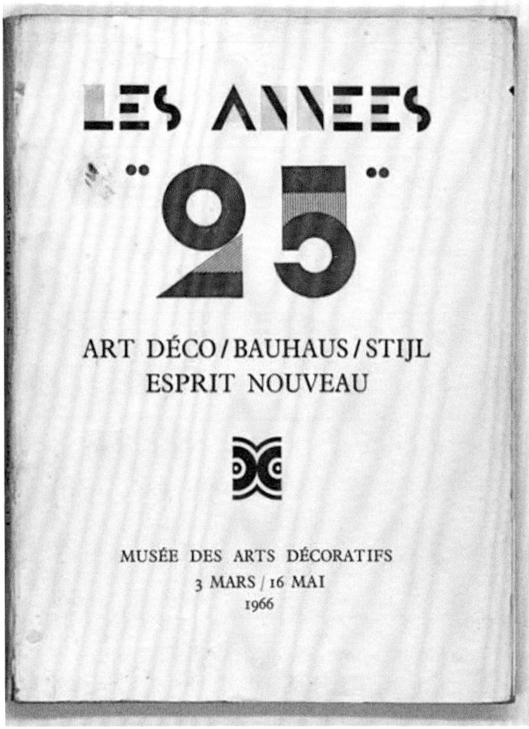

One of the earliest uses of the term "Art Deco" came in 1966, when the Musée des Art Décoratifs in Paris staged an exhibition called *Les Années "25": Art Déco/Bauhaus/Stijl/Esprit Nouveau*, as seen on the cover of the exhibition catalog.

developed as young people viewed it as a carefree, sophisticated era with great movies and fabulous clothes.[9] Finally, the renewed appreciation of Art Deco led to the establishment of Art Deco societies around the world; as Art Deco is a truly international style, societies exist in Shanghai, Melbourne, Durban, Tehran, Toulouse, Buenos Aires, and elsewhere. The Chicago Art Deco Society began in 1982.[10]

The touchstone for this revival was that 1925 Paris exhibition, where many people got their first look at some of the motifs that would come to be considered classic Art Deco. The Parisian designs could be rather elaborate, but when the style crossed the Atlantic, American designers cultivated a form that emphasized sleek lines; new materials like chrome, Bakelite, Vitrolite, and Formica; and eventually a high-tech spirit. This later phase of Art Deco is often called "Streamline Moderne." It has also been usefully characterized as a "decorative machine aesthetic."[11] In 1930 the American architect and author W. Francklyn Paris observed, "The apostles of '*Art Nouveau*,' back in 1900, sought and found their inspiration in plant life. Everything was sinuous, pliant, supple, curly, and curved. Today, the torch bearers find their inspiration in the machine. It was suddenly discovered that the automobile, the ocean liner, the locomotive, the printing press, the unadorned office building, have a power of inspiration quite as aesthetic as any garden. How ungainly, how positively ugly was the outline of the first automobiles—and now how sleek, how graceful, how aesthetically satisfying!"[12]

As Paris pointed out, one place Art Deco streamlining particularly caught on was the railroads, especially on prestige routes like Chicago–New York. Surprisingly, wrapping a steam locomotive in a sleek shroud (one critic called it an "inverted bathtub") did not do much to increase speed or save fuel, but railroad executives still favored the look. As one designer put it, if "you put an exciting new streamlined engine on the front, I am willing to bet that my train will be packed and make money." A railroad official said streamlining didn't lower air resistance, it lowered "passenger resistance."[13]

Some analysts have argued that the zigzag phase and the streamline phase are different enough to be two styles, but Bevis Hillier said: "Although there was a great and acknowledged difference in character between the twenties and thirties, it is wise to use one name—Art Deco—to cover the art of both decades, to emphasize the continuity and essential unity of the style."[14] To accommodate the many phases and features of Art Deco, Hillier has recommended it be thought of as a "hybrid" style. For François Mathey, author of the catalog for *Les Années "25,"* "More than a date, 1925 is a state of mind [*état d'esprit*]."[15] Mathey also points out that art movements in Belgium, the Netherlands, Austria, and Germany that were contemporaneous with the 1925 exposition tended to be less florid than French Art Deco and more in line with a "functional rigor" with "social mission," yet they were aligned with the novel aesthetic.

Objects from the Paris show (along with replicas) toured in America soon after the exhibition and made a strong impression, but even before that, "moderne" precursors of Art Deco had been seen in the United States. The Newark Museum, for example, began displaying European avant-garde decorative arts as early as 1912.

In the 1920s, Americans thought of "art moderne" as an import from France, which it largely was, but similar movements flourished in Scandinavia, Germany, central Europe, and Vienna. The Wiener Werkstätte (Viennese Workshops) led by Josef Hoffman were a major player in this development. In 1922 the multitalented progressive architect Joseph Urban of Vienna brought to New York a large number of representative works by the Werkstätte modernists. *The New York Times* described the exhibition as "charming, new, and original" and "a fine selection of silver and metal work, enamels, ceramics, laces, jewelry, silks, wall paper and many other beautiful things."[16] A few months later, the show was taken to Chicago. Eleanor Jewett, writing in the *Chicago Tribune*, was ecstatic, commenting on the "lovely paintings" and "most attractive lamps." She also noted the "books, exquisitely bound; little figures that enchant one by their delicate grace" while adding, "there are bowls, too, and jars, and plates and laces of cobweb finesse."[17]

Josef Hoffman had also been involved with a Viennese design initiative called the Wiener Secession (Vienna Secession). As early as 1927, two young Chicagoans, Robert Switzer and Harold O. Warner, opened a store called Secession Ltd., which was the first in the city to sell "moderne" furniture, glass, fabrics, pottery, and so on.[18] Some critics of the day went so far as to interpret the styles seen at the 1925 Paris exposition as derivative of the earlier Austrian and German modes. The critic Sheldon Cheney commented the French were "adapters of the Viennese thing."[19]

An often-overlooked source of the new aesthetic for American designers was the stylings of the chic new ocean liners. When asked how his father transitioned from historical styles to forward-looking ones, John Augur Holabird Jr., son of the cofounder of the Chicago architectural firm Holabird & Root, said, "I think partly being aware of what was happening in the Scandinavian countries where there were ships like the *Kungsholm* that my father took a couple of times. He said that the woodwork and the interiors had broken with tradition but had lots of ornament and design."[20] In fact, "ocean liner style" was one of the early candidates for a term to describe Art Deco, as designers who were fond of nautical motifs, like Holabird, began to employ porthole windows, rounded corners, and ship-style railings.[21] In France this nautical aesthetic was known as "Style Paquebot."

Although Art Deco was prevalent in the dwellings of the moneyed and in luxurious ocean liners, it surged into middle-class homes in the form of art glass and glazed tiles, as well as affordable appliances like Hotpoint toasters, Sunbeam coffee makers, Streamliner radios, and Hamilton electric calendar clocks, all of which happened to be designed and manufactured in Chicago.[22]

At the same time, American designers were beginning to employ elements derived from Native American cultures in the West, as well as Aztec and Mayan motifs (the term "Mesoamerican" was generally used) now considered Art Deco or proto–Art Deco. Although Art Deco conceived of itself as new and modern, designers saw no contradiction in employing historical motifs, as long as they were inspirations for decoration. As art historian Oriana Baddeley has said, the "geometric forms and patterns, seen as characteristics of the art of ancient Mexico, found new life in the architecture and design of the 1920s and 1930s."[23] Historian Lucy Fischer has explained how Art Deco designers used Egyptian, African, Japanese, Aztec, and Chinese imagery as "part of the style's relentless dedication to decoration and ornament—a trend that flew in the face of more austere schools of modernism."[24] A major precursor of Art Deco was that most irrepressibly American of architects and designers, Frank Lloyd Wright. Well before World War I, he was fashioning, especially in his art glass and ceramic tiles, geometric patterns and motifs often described as prefiguring Art Deco. Wright's design for Midway Gardens (1913), a large entertainment complex (now demolished) in Chicago's Hyde Park neighborhood, has often been cited as a precursor of Art Deco. Of this building, architectural historian Paul Kruty has commented that we can "revel in its extraordinary vitality in the service of an architecture of pleasure and rejoice that it served as well as an inspiration to the decorated modernism that came after . . . Midway Gardens is the spiritual progenitor of the Chicago buildings that follow."[25] So it's possible a version of the style would have arisen in America even if the Paris show never happened. But it would have been a different version, without the European touches that made American Art Deco such an attractive hybrid style.

"SKYSCRAPERVILLE"

In the first two decades of the twentieth century, the population of Chicago almost doubled. Between 1918 and 1928, more buildings were constructed in Chicago than in all the previous years of its history, and downtown land values soared. Thanks to new building techniques, such as pneumatic riveting, improved joist designs, and reinforced concrete piles, the speed and durability of new construction were increasing. In the 1880s and 1890s, Chicago architects invented the skyscraper, but in 1893 the civic authorities, fearful that so many tall buildings would create an oppressive cityscape and plunge downtown into darkness, put a height limit on new buildings, which, along with a major economic depression, put the brakes on skyscraper construction.

Is there a difference between a tall building and a skyscraper? As renowned architect Robert A. M. Stern has commented, "the great Chicago architects were the ones who were quick to comprehend the differences between tall buildings . . . and skyscrapers, between buildings that are merely exceptionally vertical and those that are capable of exhibiting their height with pride and power."[26] And yet that sounds a little vague. So just how tall is a skyscraper? In August 1929, *American Builder* magazine defined a skyscraper as anything of ten or more stories, although it admitted that this estimate was "hardly more than relative; for while it conjures visions of the high buildings in some of our larger cities, a 15-story building in a smaller city is much more of a skyscraper than is a 20-story building in New York's towering financial center."[27] The journal counted 384 buildings in Chicago of ten to twenty stories and 65 of twenty-one stories or more, for a total of 449. That was second in the nation to New York—which had five and a half times as many.

Skyscrapers can be measured in more than height, though. Developers were typically no-nonsense types who didn't build just to go high; they built to make money. As early as the 1890s, a critic named Barr Ferree said, "Current American architecture is not a matter of art, but of business. A building must pay or there will be no investor ready with the money to meet its cost."[28] Chicago's Art Deco towers might have been stylish, but they also had to be profit machines.

So what did an Art Deco skyscraper cost? Chicago's Merchandise Mart cost $38 million (around $900 million today) and the Central Post Office from $16 to $21 million, but they were atypical because they were long and deep as well as tall. The Board of Trade Building came in at $11 million, the Daily News Building cost $8 million, and the price tag on the Mundelein Center was just $2.5 million. In 1929 the *Architectural Record* compared building costs in various US cities. Using New York City as a baseline of 100, they reported Chicago at 88. Many cities, including Boston, Buffalo, Philadelphia, Cleveland, St. Louis, and others, were higher. The prices for building materials (85) were especially good in Chicago; a few years later, another study showed that labor costs in Chicago were pretty much in line with those in other large American cities.[29]

In 1923 the city adopted a setback ordinance that allowed taller skyscrapers if their profiles were "set back" in stages as they rose. At their highest point, buildings could occupy just one-fourth of the area of their site—a recipe for a tower. Chicago's setback rule, like others, was modeled on the one established in New York City in 1916 due to concerns that such mammoth skyscraper blocks obscured airflow and sunlight, which was not only unsightly but detrimental to the health of office workers. Chicago lawmakers might have waited to see how that ordinance worked before instituting their own. Once they did, Chicago effectively no longer had a height restriction and the city soon boasted the Wrigley Building, the Chicago Temple, the London Guarantee & Accident Building, the Straus Building, and the Jewelers Building. These setback skyscrapers were not Art Deco; they were mostly in the Neoclassical and Beaux-Arts styles celebrated in Chicago's famous 1893 World's Columbian Exposition, a.k.a. the "White City." The setback ordinance is the reason many Chicago Art Deco skyscrapers have similar profiles.

At the same time as establishing the setback rule, city planners, in order to rationalize new construction, divided Chicago into five "volume districts." These guidelines, in an effort to control density, regulated not just the height of new buildings but also their bulk (horizontal expanse). The district bounded by Chicago Avenue on the north, 22nd Street on the south, Halsted Street on the west, and Lake Michigan on the east permitted the tallest structures—hence the concentration of Art Deco towers in the area, which the *Chicago Tribune* at the time named "Skyscraperville."[30]

As spectacular as the White City and the buildings it inspired were, critics (such as Louis Sullivan) were disappointed they did not point the way to an innovative future and did not light a path toward a distinctively American architectural aesthetic. In 1922 the architecture critic Thomas Tallmadge said the attempt to "create an American style has proved to be a failure," and a thick survey from 1928, *The American Architecture of To-day*, contains essentially no buildings we would consider Art Deco, or even very modern for that matter. But Art Deco architecture came on fast. One of the curious things about Chicago's Art Deco skyscrapers is that a good amount of the inspiration behind them came from a building that was never constructed.

It began in June 1922, when the *Chicago Tribune* announced that the "World's Greatest Newspaper" would be holding a competition for a new office skyscraper, with prize money totaling $100,000. Architects from all over the world were invited to submit proposals, and more than 250 did. The winner was a Gothic-tinged tower (complete with gargoyles) modeled on the Tour de Beurre (1506) at the cathedral of Rouen, by the team of John Mead Howells and Raymond Hood of New York. If it was somewhat backward-looking, Tribune Tower has since become a beloved landmark.

The second prize went to Eliel Saarinen, then of Finland, who was assisted by his Chicago-based partners Dwight G. Wallace and Bertell Grenman. This entry was something else altogether—a spare, soaring tower that wowed contemporary architects, newspaper critics, and the general public. Writing in *Architectural Forum* in 1930, Charles G. Loring said Saarinen's drawing "inaugurated an office building cult from the Great Lakes to the Rio Grande."[31] At the same time, the no longer pessimistic Tallmadge wrote that in its design "lay the solution of the skyscraper, a veritable philosopher's stone that would transmute the dross of eclecticism into the gold of new architecture."[32] His comment came at about the same time as the construction of 333 North Michigan, which had little about it that could be called "eclectic." The Tribune Tower used Gothic motifs; Saarinen's building—and 333 North Michigan—didn't. A new movement was being born, one that rejected buildings based on European historical models, such as Gothic and Beaux-Arts. As Art Deco historian Alistair Duncan expressed it, "All at once Neoclassical entablatures, columns, flying buttresses, ogives, architraves, gargoyles and all the standard Beaux-Arts motifs were passé, stylistic remnants of bygone architectural eras."[33]

Looking back from the perspective of the late 1930s, Columbia University architecture professor Talbot F. Hamlin said the path toward modernism had been cleared by its application first in domestic use. Speaking of the 1925 Paris exhibition, he said, "without the flood of 'modernism' which followed that exposition in furniture, lighting fixtures, and so on, today's readiness to consider and adapt new forms (slight as that may be) would have been impossible. Commerce taught the buying public what forward-looking architects had known for some time, that archaeological architecture was dead."[34]

Eliel Saarinen's entry placed second in the 1922 *Chicago Tribune* competition for a new Tribune Tower and was never built, but it was a revelation for American architects who saw it as the path forward in skyscraper design. Library of Congress Prints and Photographs Division, LC-DIG-ppmsca-51973.

"A DISTINCTIVE AMERICAN ARCHITECTURE"

If the initial inspiration for the new style in the United States came from France, Americans quickly showed the world what could be done with the "moderne" aesthetic. As curator and historian Mike Hope has said, "Art Deco architecture as developed in America became the first true American style that ultimately was exported around the world."[35]

In the summer of 1928, the architectural critic John Taylor Boyd Jr. visited an exhibition of the Chicago Architectural League. "Among the exhibits," he reported in *Architectural Record*, "were seen designs of projects for the city plan and photographs of such work already completed and of buildings like some of the newer office tower buildings near the river. . . . In all this work, the characteristic that struck me as finest in this Chicago architecture is its big bold scale. Better than any other group, the Chicago architects seem to sense the big scale of the modern city. . . . One could never apply to it the words 'too delicate,' 'finicky,' 'prettified,' 'sentimental,' which describe only too aptly much contemporary New York design."[36] (Take that, Big Apple!) A year later, Edward Alden Jewell of *The New York Times*, reviewing the new work of Holabird & Root, echoed the sentiment that the Windy City was leading the search for a tasteful "moderne" aesthetic: "If we are not careful, Chicago is going to get far ahead of us in this matter, for a good many of our recent New York structures confess an urgent need of pruning. Holabird and Root offer an object lesson in taste."[37] Finally, in 1930 a Northwestern professor named Lawrence Martin argued that Americans were best in architecture, "for we are a 'nation of builders.'" He considered Chicago's Art Deco towers the finest of the new buildings and complained only that there were too few because some architects were still looking backward.[38]

In 1929, Louis La Beaume, a director of the American Institute of Architects, complained, "A diligent student may make the equivalent of the grand tour of Europe and familiarize himself with the culture of a dozen races throughout a period of century 2,000 years without a passport,—without even a twinge of seasickness. This is the architecture of America, but what of American architecture?" And yet, he saw modern American architecture as finally emerging:

> If our old stodgy habits are changing, if we are beginning to detect a new crispness and terseness, a new simplicity and directness in the design of our small as well as of our large buildings, we may seek for the cause in two factors. First, we are living in a crisper, speedier, smarter time; and, second, client and architect are more nearly one and the same than they ever were before. The young architect of today feels and reflects the tempo of his generation. . . . As a plagiarist with a bad conscience but at the same time with an earnest desire to reform, I would say that the American architect should have full faith in the essential virtues of the American character, and that he should "be himself."[39]

Fittingly, the article in which he was quoted was titled "A Distinctive American Architecture."

BUILDERS, ENGINEERS, AND ARTISTS

The beauty of Chicago's Art Deco skyscrapers can also blind us to another of their noteworthy features: they were feats of engineering. In 1928 structural engineer Col. William A. Starrett published *Skyscrapers and the Men Who Build Them*, an illustrated volume that explains how such tall buildings were erected. The book covers, among other things, planning, design, costs, zoning, excavation, foundations (floating, hardpan, and rock), pile drivers (steam and pneumatic), power-driven gang saws, bracing, derricks, stonework, terra-cotta, labor, and exterior and interior decoration, with the chief innovations being in the areas of steel and reinforced concrete. Three other essential inventions were structural steel, handheld pneumatic riveting machines—pneumatically riveted joints were tighter and more rigid than the old-fashioned handmade ones[40]—and swift and safe electric elevators. (Starrett says, "even the sturdy calves of our unpampered forefathers balked at climbing more than six stories."[41])

The Northwest Tower in Wicker Park under construction. In the 1920s, technological innovations, especially in the areas of steel and reinforced concrete, made construction work faster and safer. Courtesy of the Robey Hotel.

One of the more impressive, if rarely recognized, innovations of Chicago's architects and engineers was in caisson technology (caissons are the tall underground pillars that hold up buildings).[42] Unlike in Manhattan, where the soil is undergirded by solid bedrock that gives excellent support to tall buildings, Chicago rests on a mushy goop nicknamed Chicago blue clay that's a challenge for builders. While New York architects erected their towers on unshakable stone, Chicagoans had to build theirs on something approximating gelatin. But there is bedrock beneath Chicago; it's just far down (at about one hundred feet). And at a lesser depth (seventy feet or so), there is a sturdy gray silty clay known as hardpan that can support buildings as tall as forty stories.

In the early 1890s engineer William Sooy Smith devised the "Chicago caisson," a hand-dug cylinder that flared at the bottom in a bell shape and was filled with concrete. Caissons were more commonly straight-sided, and these were also used in Chicago. Early caissons were used to support the northern half of the Monadnock Building (1891). The first use of caissons for the foundation of an entire building was the Methodist Book Concern on West Washington Street (1899). Some Chicago caissons rest on hardpan; many go down to bedrock.[43] Some of the Art Deco skyscrapers that use such caissons are the Chicago Board of Trade Building, the Buckingham Building, 333 North Michigan, the Chicago Motor Club, One North La Salle, the La Salle-Wacker Building, and the Field Building.

Directing the construction of a skyscraper was like planning a military operation. In fact, Col. Starrett's brother Paul, a builder who put up some of the most prestigious skyscrapers of the era, made just that comparison in his autobiography: "Every building job is different from every other, just as every battle in a campaign is different. Nothing is standardized in the building business, and the human element is larger than in any other industry. When we start a building we draw up a schedule, giving the time allotted to each branch of the work, with starting and completion dates, and showing how the time for each trade interlocks with other trades. This schedule is both written and graphic. . . . Subcontractors and manufacturers are required to carry on divisions of the work to fit these schedules."[44]

While focused on logistics, Col. Starrett was not blind to aesthetic considerations. He noted that while

Chicago's setback ordinance aimed to keep buildings from blocking the sunlight, they also encouraged an architectural form of "intrinsic beauty."[45] His esteem echoes the praise of New York–based skyscraper pioneer Henry Wiley Corbett in 1921: "The square-topped flat-roofed packing box building is a thing of the past (fortunately), and we now have the step-back skyline. . . . Buildings in the future will not be designed merely as 'fronts' but will be studied from all angles, even that of an aviator. Architectural design has moved from a two-dimension stage (where it never should have been) to a three-dimension stage (where real design always was)."[46]

The "architectural geologist" Raymond Wiggers, in his book *Chicago in Stone and Clay*, describes what he calls "the Grand Art Deco formula": "a huge expanse of the limestone above, literally a monolithic mass, footed by a crystalline rock type that is a darker, more detailed, and sometimes a more subversive contrast to the beige uniformity above it."[47] This facing on this base, Col. Starrett writes, is almost always of granite four to eight inches thick. "Architects," he says, "have found that the combination of granite and some other stone makes a pleasing and dignified façade."[48]

Most Chicago Art Deco skyscrapers are made of what is usually called Indiana or Bedford limestone but is technically Salem Limestone, or biocalcarenite, mined from Indiana quarries such as Dark Hollow, P. M. & B., Hoosier, Walsh, Doyle, Eureka, and Peerless. Wiggers comments that "there's so much of this famous Hoosier export in Chicago that the city could plausibly be renamed New Indiana."[49] In a 1929 advertisement in *Architectural Forum*, the Indiana Limestone Company proudly listed new Chicago buildings that used its product: "'333,' the Palmolive Building, the Medinah Athletic Club, Willoughby Tower, Chicago Daily News Building and Foreman National Bank." John Augur Holabird Jr. explained that limestone especially suited Chicago buildings: "It was a marvelous exterior material for Chicago because the temperature in Chicago goes from 110 in the summer to 10 below in the winter, and the material has to be flexible."[50] Indiana limestone was also used for sculpture.

The American architect Bertram Goodhue, who died in 1924, was considered a progressive in his day; the *Journal of the American Institute of Architects* called him "The First True Modern."[51] Goodhue said a successful modern building had to have a visionary architect, of course, but that was not enough. He argued the need for two more contributors: an artist to paint murals and a sculptor to supply reliefs and other sculpturesque touches. Statues in the round were not used much, but bas-reliefs were pervasive in Chicago's Art Deco skyscrapers. As historian Aliki Economides has written, "the bas-relief was both an archaic sculptural form revived with particular enthusiasm as part of a 'modern' aesthetic, and one of the most common, if not the *defining* features of architecture; a building's characterization as 'Art Deco' being dependent to a significant extent on the sculpted ornament animating its surfaces."[52]

Goodhue's comment is a reminder of the importance of decoration in Chicago's Art Deco skyscrapers. In a vital, but overlooked, essay from 1932 titled "The Question of Decoration," the muralist Hildreth Meiere, whose work adorned several Art Deco buildings, said, "To my mind, decoration is that which gives color or texture, scale of pattern or interest, which is used, whether functionally or not, because it gives pleasure or expression. An architect instinctively employs it because he is an artist who designs for aesthetic enjoyment as well as a builder who must build adequately for physical needs. . . . To choose a certain brick for a wall is to choose decoration; to design a terrazzo floor is to start ornamenting. The extreme Left Wing Modernists have confused decoration with historic ornament."[53]

As Alistair Duncan has pointed out, "Art Deco ornamentation was concentrated principally on that part of a building seen and used by most occupants, i.e., its entranceway—exterior grillework, doors, vestibule, and bank of elevators. Often a sumptuous combination of stone, brick, terracotta, and metal transformed an otherwise bland structure into a great source of civic pride."[54] It can be argued that it's not the architectural form that earns most buildings the Art Deco label, but the ornamental decoration, although it's important to remember that the previous generation of Chicago skyscraper architects, such as Daniel Burnham and, especially, Louis Sullivan, were masters of

62 PENCIL POINTS FOR FEBRUARY, 1931

BRONZE..

NICKEL SILVER..OR IRON..*but*

ever faithful to Architect's Designs

On this page are three examples of recent General Bronze jobs . . . Three types of elevator doors — three different styles of designs — three different metals.

The doors of the Chicago Daily News Building are of modern *nickel silver.* The vertical design gives an effect of height and loftiness. Metal strips on each side accent this idea . . .

The design of 1 La Salle Street shows the use of *bronze* at its best. Fineness of scale, of line and of shading — such as bronze can achieve . . .

The Foshay Tower doors are *cast iron* with a classically wrought design. The bas relief representation of the building — worked into the door — is *bronze* — an effective combination for contrast . . .

Foshay Tower, Minneapolis, Minn.—Wrought Iron Elevator Doors with cast bronze inserts. *Architects:* Magney & Tussler.

Chicago Daily News—Elevator Doors, nickel silver. *Architects:* Holabird & Root.

1 La Salle Street, Chicago, Ill. — Elevator Doors, bronze. *Architects:* K. M. Vitzthum Co.

A NEW ENGINEERING SERVICE

Both with the older and modern architectural metals, General Bronze has had wide experience. This construction and technique experience is available through the new *"Metal Engineering Service."* It is a *practical* and personal service rendered from our New York and Minneapolis offices. Architects are sincerely invited to avail themselves of this new General Bronze department.

"DISTINCTIVE PRODUCTIONS IN ALL METALS"

GENERAL BRONZE CORPORATION

480 HANCOCK STREET · LONG ISLAND CITY, N. Y.

Many independent companies supplied fixtures for Art Deco buildings, as seen in this magazine advertisement, which features two Chicago buildings. Author's collection.

ornamentation. Like the Art Deco designers, they relied on independent companies who specialized in providing such details (elevators, bank-teller cages, mosaic floors, murals, bas-reliefs, and so on). It's not ornamentation per se that makes a building Art Deco, it's the style of the decoration.

In Chicago's Art Deco skyscrapers, much effort went into the lobbies. Elevator doors, with their large expanses, were catnip to interior designers, and some of the most spectacular Art Deco work in Chicago buildings can be found on them. Interior grilles, such as the large coverings for vents and radiators, also boasted such treatment. In 1931 the Harrington & King Perforating Company held a design competition for a radiator grille to "increase the variety of designs in the field of Modern Art." The winner was an imaginative "moderne" Art Deco design. The company made grilles of steel, brass, bronze, stainless iron, aluminum, and Monel metal (a corrosion-resistant nickel-copper alloy).

Chicago's Art Deco architects did not necessarily retain their own artistic teams to adorn their buildings. Independent companies would supply terra-cotta or brass and bronze embellishments, and freelance artists practiced architectural decoration. For example, the bronze elevator doors of One North La Salle and the Chicago Daily News Building were done by the General Bronze Corporation of Long Island City, New York. The National Terra Cotta Company, based in New York City, represented the many manufacturers of this popular material; three of the biggest were in Chicago. One of their free pamphlets was "Color in Architecture," which featured a bank by Louis Sullivan. The Brasco Manufacturing Company of Chicago specialized in bronze storefronts. Also, deriving inspiration from previous styles of ornament was seen as almost unavoidable and certainly not to be derided. As architect and writer Rayne Adams wrote in 1929, "the vocabulary of the arts is a great granary and even the most original of men use and play with symbols and forms which were old when Memnon first spoke."[55]

In addition to ornamental features, dozens and dozens of Chicago companies supplied the elements of a skyscraper (and most other buildings). These elements might seem trifling, but Art Deco designers and architects took them seriously. Issues of *Architectural Forum* contain pages of advertisements for Chicago firms offering such items as interior paint, stucco, tile, bronze storefronts, face brick, locks and door checks, switch plates, mortar pigment, wood paneling and trim, radiator enclosures, flooring, lighting equipment, doors, partitions, mirrors, and bathroom fixtures. These companies gladly sent out free pamphlets and brochures to induce builders to use their products.

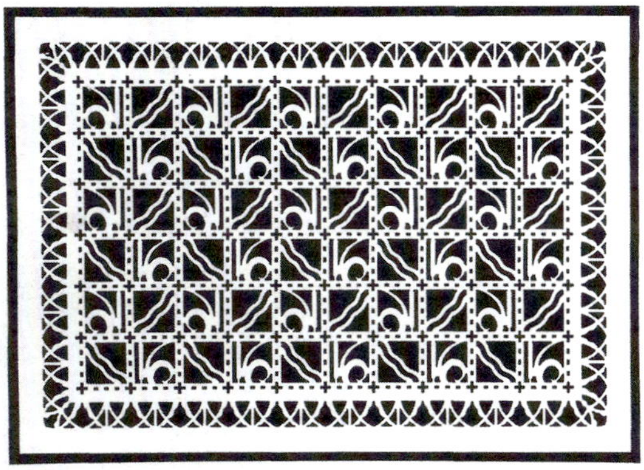

Grilles are often one of the most interesting design features of Art Deco skyscrapers. The Chicago-based Harrington & King Perforating Company, which made grilles of a variety of metals, held a design competition in 1931 for a radiator grille. The winner was an innovative "moderne" Art Deco design. Author's collection.

THE SKYSCRAPER ARCHITECTS

The skyscrapers featured in these pages were built by nine architectural firms, but two firms stand out as the most prolific. Holabird & Root designed six, and five were the work of Graham, Anderson, Probst & White (GAPW).[56] In Chicago, you can't escape the buildings of Holabird & Root. The firm erected skyscrapers in some of the most prominent locations in the city. There's the riverfront Chicago Daily News Building. There's 333 North Michigan, which is visible the entire length of upper Michigan Avenue. And, at the northern culmination of the Mag Mile, there's the Palmolive Building, which once boasted a two-billion-candlepower beacon, the brightest in the world. On La Salle Street, the firm put up the ultra-conspicuous Chicago Board of Trade Building at the southern end of the canyon and, at its northern entrance, the stately La Salle-Wacker Building, once known as "The Gateway to Finance." Ironically, according to John Root, John Holabird was never satisfied with their finished products and "found it difficult to walk downtown because he had to avoid passing so many of his designs."[57] As for GAPW, Clifford Noonan, who worked for them for thirty years, described the prolific company in this manner:

> Mr. Graham was the business-getter, the developer, who had the contacts that were nationwide, maybe international. After the designs were determined, after the preliminaries were approved by the owner, that was the area where Mr. Graham functioned with the designers to develop a scheme to solve the owner's problem. After that was finalized—what we would call the design development stage today—it was then transferred over to Mr. Probst, who was responsible for production with the engineering, for all necessary construction details and construction documents, they were prepared based on the approved sketches. And after they were completed, they were turned over to Mr. White and bids were taken. They were either negotiated or advertised or competitive bidding was used depending upon the client or what the problems were at the time. And then after the bids were submitted, they were opened in the presence of Mr. White and Mr. Graham, and an award was made based upon whatever was to the owner's advantage at that time. And from then on Mr. White handled the progress of the work until the completion of the job.[58]

The age of the Art Deco skyscraper in Chicago was brief. Construction on 333 North Michigan, the first, began in the summer of 1927, and the last one, the Field Building, began welcoming tenants in 1933. The effects of the Great Depression were dire. Skyscraper building ended, not to be revived until the 1950s. The staff of Holabird & Root shrunk from a high of 350 employees to 7 or 8.[59] The value of new construction in Chicago in 1928 was about $315 million; in 1933 it was less than $4 million.[60] But in those scant six years, Chicago builders put up no fewer than twenty Art Deco skyscrapers (along with, of course, many smaller buildings), a testament to the prosperity of the 1920s.

Although these Chicago architects produced magnificent buildings, they are not exactly household names. As Patricia Bayer wrote, "Art Deco is not an architecture of personalities, of star architects. It is an architecture of the buildings themselves, of their inherent yet overt qualities and of their spirit, energy and immediate visual impact, not of their internal structures, services, floor plans, and front and side elevations. Few members of the general public in the West can name an Art Deco architect, but most are more than familiar, for instance, with the Empire State Building."[61] Or, as Mike Hope put it, "Whilst most people can name perhaps one of the iconic products of Art Deco architecture, can anyone name the architects? Certainly . . . the cult of the superstar architect seemed to skip the Art Deco period."[62] The reason for such obscurity might be that nearly all the Chicago Art Deco skyscrapers were designed by teams, not by a single individual. In the Jazz Age, American architects increasingly worked with ever-larger crews that included contractors, designers, and engineers. Holabird & Root adopted what's been called a "collaborative approach" that involved landscape designers, sculptors, mural painters, interior designers, and so on.[63]

Also, the names at the heads of architectural firms were often not the architects who designed the buildings. The partners usually filled specific functions that were not necessarily design related. In the late 1930s, the architectural critic Henry-Russell Hitchcock said, "It is impossible to say whether many of the outstanding architects of America, since the development of an office organization, could have designed a building: it is very clear that few of them have ever directly done so."[64] At GAPW, for example, Probst was head of the drafting room, White dealt with the subcontractors, and Graham was the persuasive salesman who brought in the business. In 1938, architect Russell F. Whitehead commented, "As the tendency towards big organizations grew, the creative artist at their head was often obscured and came to be considered by rival architects as 'just a factory manager.'"[65]

During the Art Deco era, the head designer for

GAPW was Alfred Shaw. He did the designs for three Art Deco skyscrapers: the Civic Opera House, the Merchandise Mart, and the Field Building. (Shaw also designed the original McCormick Place, Marshall Field's downtown department store, the Continental Plaza Hotel, and the interior of the Museum of Science and Industry.) Meanwhile, also for GAPW, Charles Beersman designed the Wrigley Building and the Foreman State National Bank Building, and Mario Schiavoni did the Shedd Aquarium.[66]

Architectural firms also made critical use of another type of specialist—the engineer. William Le Baron Jenney, often credited as the father of the skyscraper in the 1880s, was more renowned as an engineer than as an architect. Engineers of Chicago's Art Deco skyscrapers include Verne O. McClurg (Chicago Board of Trade Building and the Buckingham Building), Magnus Gunderson (Merchandise Mart), Frank A. Randall (Lawson House YMCA), and the prolific Frank Elam Brown, who engineered some twenty Chicago buildings in the 1920s, including the Art Deco towers 333 North Michigan, the Chicago Motor Club, and the Chicago Daily News Building. In 1929 *The Chicagoan* magazine paid homage to the era's engineers, "who have created the swift and shining civilization in which we live. They are the dreamers and builders; the tamers of lightning, the magicians of the atom, the gallant riders of the machine. They are the modern intellectuals."[67]

In the Jazz Age, Chicago's power brokers called their metropolis a "City of True Dreams."[68] On the last day of 1929, James Simpson, chairman of the Chicago Plan Commission, listed thirty-six major civic improvement projects that had been completed during 1929 alone. Among them were a new outer drive, the straightening of the Chicago River, the extension of Wacker Drive, completion of the Clark Street Bridge and the Adler Planetarium, the widening of thoroughfares, and the signing of a contract for the establishment of the Museum of Science and Industry. Despite the dismal economic atmosphere so recently brought on by the Great Depression, Chicago, he said, "took a big stride toward its ambition of becoming the world's premier city."[69]

The sightseer who follows the Art Deco trail in Chicago's Loop will experience a combination of grandeur, technology, history, and inspiration. The concluding remarks of Col. William A. Starrett are both stirring and saddening. Stirring because they are filled with a kind of naive but inspirational American can-do spirit and saddening because it's difficult to imagine a commentator writing them in our anxious times: "Modern ingenuity, having visioned the possibilities of vast mechanical accomplishment, is whirling us on toward an inscrutable destiny. . . . [T]he whole effort is toward making human life easier and happier, freeing it from exhausting and inefficient toil, and giving to every one a better balance between leisure and useful occupation. . . . Destiny beckons us to a future that we feel is to be ever brighter."

A NOTE ON TERMINOLOGY AND APPROACH

It can be difficult to decide what a building should be called because the name given at its opening is often not the one it bears today. For example, the Chicago Daily News Building is currently Two North Riverside Plaza, the Trustees System Service Building is now Century Tower, and the Buckingham Building has had five names. And future owners may well rename these or other skyscrapers. For that reason, I try to use the original names, often sourced to the *AIA Guide to Chicago.*

Importantly, this is not a book solely about architecture. As mentioned, some significant artists and sculptors played important roles. But more centrally, each building has a tale to tell—not only about the structure itself but also about its cultural context. For example, the chapter on the Daily News Building discusses the vast role played by newspapers in the 1920s and '30s. The chapter on the Chicago Motor Club describes the escalating impact of the automobile, while the one on the Powhatan discusses the growing popularity of apartment living. In addition, some intriguing and significant personalities were connected to these structures. I cover the buildings in roughly chronological order. Finally, a few myths have become attached to some of these buildings, and I aim to dispel them.

Nº. 1

333 NORTH MICHIGAN

HOLABIRD & ROOT, 1928

333 North Michigan, which began accepting tenants in the spring of 1928, was Chicago's first Art Deco skyscraper. And, of the skyscrapers in this book, it might have the best location at the southern end of the DuSable Bridge, which carries Michigan Avenue, the Windy City's grandest boulevard, across the Chicago River. In February 1929, *Architectural Record* said the building had a "sentinel quality."[1] Because the bridge is slightly angled to the east, when a viewer anywhere on Michigan Avenue north of the river looks to the south, 333 appears to be right smack in the center of the Magnificent Mile. This also means the people *inside* the building have unparalleled views to the north of the throughfare and beyond.

The site is a component of what skyscraper expert Kheir Al-Kodmany has called Chicago's "Grand Gateway"—the node at the junction of the Chicago River and Michigan Avenue. It consists, he says, of several exceptional buildings in addition to 333 North Michigan: the London Guarantee & Accident Building, the Wrigley Building, Tribune Tower, and the Medinah Athletic Club. Of all these treasured buildings, however, only 333 is Art Deco; the others, though built

333 North Michigan might have the best location of any Chicago Art Deco skyscraper. This 1920s view of Chicago's "Grand Gateway" shows 333, the London Guarantee & Accident Building, the Wrigley Building, Tribune Tower, and the Medinah Athletic Club.

Opposite: In the early 1930s, 333 North Michigan, at the request of the architects, sported its address in illuminated numbers. HB-01291-B, Chicago History Museum, Hedrich-Blessing Collection.

at around the same time, look back to historical models.[2] 333 was deliberately, and forcefully, "moderne."

333 North Michigan was designed by the team of John Augur Holabird (1886–1945) and John Wellborn Root Jr. (1887–1963). Both were sons of distinguished Chicago architects of the previous generation, William Holabird (1854–1923), who was the partner of Martin Roche, and John Wellborn Root Sr. (1850–1891), who was the partner of Daniel Burnham. The sons met in Paris, where they were students at the École des Beaux-Arts, and it was there the pair absorbed much of the new modernistic styles then in bloom. The firm was known as Holabird & Roche until the death of Martin Roche in 1927, after which it became Holabird & Root. Between 1883 and 1945, the firm completed more than 7,500 commissions.

In late fall 1929 an exhibition of their work was held at the Architectural League of New York, of which a reviewer wrote, "Embodying a distinctly new note and a fresh expression in architectural design, work of these young architects is making one of the most marked contributions to the present development of a distinctly American architectural style. Their work shows a marked appreciation of scale and proportion, a consummate understanding of the value of masses, and an unusual appreciation of the importance of a proper relation between window spacing and wall surfaces. Their buildings without exception possess unusual restraint and dignity, relieved by an intelligent and consistent use of appropriate ornament."[3] This flattering analysis seems to have been based on 333 North Michigan, which had opened just one year before. A few months later, *The Chicagoan* called Holabird & Root "leaders of a group of Chicago architects whose work during the past few years has been an amazing efflorescence of progress in a profession whose traditions are strongly conservative. The towers of Chicago which have spired up so rapidly, especially in the Michigan Avenue district around and north of the great bridge—the special field of Holabird and Root—form a new wonder of the world."[4] The architects were also part of the team of developers; in a way, they were building the skyscraper for themselves. They moved their offices there—all 175 people—shortly after it opened, as did some other architectural firms. While Holabird & Root has since moved from 333, today it is considered the oldest architectural firm in Chicago.[5]

Compared to its neighbors, 333 stands out for its clean vertical lines, its forthright profile, and its discreet ornamentation. It's considered a classic setback skyscraper, one of the first, in that it follows the mandates of Chicago's 1923 law that permitted tall buildings if they were set back in stages as they rose—hence its dramatic tower, which covers just one-fourth of the lot area. As discussed in the introduction, archi-

333

tectural historians say some of Chicago's setback skyscrapers were inspired by the influential design that the Finnish architect Eliel Saarinen submitted to the *Chicago Tribune*'s skyscraper contest. We know this to be the case for 333 because Root said so.[6]

According to architectural geologist Raymond Wiggers, this limestone skyscraper sits on a base of Morton gneiss (so called for the town in Minnesota where it's quarried), a dark stone prized for its looping patterns of black, pink, purple, and gray. Morton gneiss was formed about 3.5 billion years ago, which makes it, according to Wiggers, "one of the oldest surviving rock units on Earth, and certainly the most ancient used in American architecture." When Wiggers brings tour groups to 333, he invites them to run their fingers down the wall: "Unless they chance upon a meteorite, this will be the oldest thing they'll touch in their entire fleeting lives."[7]

The entryway of 333 is unusual because it's located on what we commonly think of as the building's side. As the *Architectural Record* reported, "Because of the relatively small area, 62 by 200 feet, economy of space demanded even greater consideration than is usual in buildings of its type; therefore the entrance and the elevator lobbies were placed in the center of the length to permit the most flexible and economical subdivisions with a minimum amount of corridor space."[8] Although the building represents Holabird & Root's first foray into the setback mode, it's remarkably assured and appropriate for the site. A triple row of recessed windows that runs all the way to the very top, 426 feet above the pavement, adds dramatic verticality to the facade, with dark terra-cotta spandrels accentuating the stripes. The verticality is made even more prominent by the absence of a cupola or cornice at the top. The large circular, or porthole, windows at the third level are a reminder that one of the expressions used in the 1920s to describe what we now call Art Deco was "ocean liner style."

The base is lined with ten storefronts that have windows framed in cast iron, as is the main entrance. Fittingly, one of the first companies to lease one of the shop spaces was a Duesenberg automobile dealer—the dashing Duesenberg being one of the classic cars of the era and a pioneer in the streamlining of automobiles, which has made them common exemplars of Art Deco. Another of the prestigious tenants was Rena Hartman, a vendor of women's clothes that had a most comfortable space for shopping. It was so capacious that after Hartman vacated in the mid-1930s, five separate stores moved into the space.

The walls of the lobby are of a type of marble called verde antico, an opulent stone from Greece noted for its deep green color and its variegated veins and spots of white quartz. The floors are of Traitel terrazzo (terrazzo is a composite material made of chips of different stones that is often used in Art Deco buildings). The Art Deco elevator doors were the work of the British-born sculptor Albert Stewart (1900–1965), who was something of a specialist in large public sculptures. The interiors of the elevators display bronze panels depicting birds. The building opened with ten elevators—four local to the lower floors and six express to the

Advertisement from an issue of *The Chicagoan* magazine in 1930. Rena Hartman, Inc., a classy vendor of women's clothes, was a prestige tenant in 333. Author's collection.

A prominent feature of 333 North Michigan is a frieze with seven-foot-tall panels by Fred Martin Torrey that depict scenes from Chicago history. Photograph by Mike Burton. CC BY-ND 2.0, https://creativecommons.org/licenses/by-nd/2.0/deed.en.

higher ones. The elevator doors are bronze, as are the stair railings, the mailbox, the window frames, and the grilles, including those on the ceiling. The rentable space of a standard floor is around 9,500 square feet, and most interior ceilings are ten feet ten inches. In the corridors the walls are wainscoted in Vermont marble to a height of seven feet.

The exterior is decorated with a frieze by the sculptor Fred Martin Torrey (1884–1967), who was a student of the famed sculptor Lorado Taft at the Art Institute of Chicago. Harriet Monroe, editor of the trailblazing magazine *Poetry*, was John Root's aunt; after admiring a Torrey sculpture of Pegasus at the Art Institute of Chicago, she introduced the sculptor to the architect.[9] The seven-foot-tall panels of Torrey's frieze, referencing early Chicago history, were called "The Portage," "La Salle Trading with the Indians," "Attack on Fort Dearborn," "Coming of the Pioneers," "The Trapper," "The Vanishing Indian," and "The Pioneer Woman."[10] They are not traditional bas-reliefs but are cut into the stone like silhouettes. A reviewer in the *American Magazine of Art* in 1928 called them "elementally simple, modernistically direct, utterly different from anything the sculptor had ever done before, completely suitable to the requirements of scale of the building which they decorate."[11]

After Chicago's Millennium Park opened in 2004, the stretch of Michigan Avenue between Randolph Street and the river, which had been somewhat overlooked, became attractive. The Wirtz family, owners of the Chicago Blackhawks, who had recently won the National Hockey League championship three times, commissioned a $50 million renovation of the recently landmarked building by Chicago architects Goettsch Partners. Both the office and retail spaces were refurbished, and the limestone was cleaned, which made the Torrey carvings shine again. In 2019 the Michigan Avenue entrance, which had been replaced with a modern-day version, was beautifully restored, complete with Art Deco replacement sconces that, if not exact copies of the originals, are, if anything, more attractive. Finally, and fittingly, a two-level Blackhawks store moved into a prime retail location, right above Fannie May candies.

If dignity was the hallmark of 333, one interior feature was practically the opposite: the twenty-fifth-floor Tavern Club, a sybaritic haven in which languorous and jaded Jazz Age men (mostly) could partake of repose, bonhomie, poker, and illegal hooch. John Root was a prime mover in the establishment of the club and made sure to construct a terrace with a splendid view. The motives of the Tavern Club (originally called

333
333
333

just "The Tavern") were the familiar ones of conviviality and support for the arts—to which was added defiance of Prohibition. Each member was assigned a private locker just large enough to hold a few bottles. The club was dedicated on June 28, 1928. The sixteen original members were all male, but women were allowed to join under certain restrictions. That Jews were admitted was something of an enlightened anomaly; it was an era of "restricted" facilities, in which Jews, because of antisemitism, were denied membership in many organizations and public facilities. Membership was capped at 550 (raised to 605 in 1970). One of the founders, Charles Collins, wrote in *The Chicagoan* about how the board of governors first considered making the place look like a proper "old English tap-room" with half-timbered decor but then reversed direction: "'Let it be modern,' we agreed; 'yes, let it even be *moderne*.'" Thus they hired the interior decorator and artist Winold Reiss, an Art Deco specialist, and gave him carte blanche. The result, according to Collins, was that the club became "the most brilliant example of modern decorative style in the country."[12]

Edgar Miller (1899–1993), who was in the 1930s one of the most famous artists not only in Chicago but in the United States, was enlisted to decorate the club with a mural. Miller's reputation was such that he was called "the blond boy Michelangelo" and "the most versatile artist in the United States." He was an accomplished painter (especially portraits) and sculptor, but his talents extended to printmaking, woodcarving, and just about anything to do with interior design. One of his most eye-catching creations was the two-story grille of lead silhouettes he did for Chicago's Trustees System Service Building (see chapter 13). In 1938 he sculpted a delightful set of seven large playful animals for the playground at the Jane Addams Homes public housing project designed by Holabird & Root.[13] His most celebrated projects were four artists' studios begun in the 1920s that the artist called "handmade homes." In 2024 the DePaul Art Museum referred to his work as "anti-modern," meaning it was "unabashedly anachronistic." He "never embraced geometric abstraction or machine age aesthetics" but "pursued a maximalist celebration of embellishment, patterns, and figurative storytelling."[14] For today's artists striving to find a "postmodern" aesthetic, he might provide much inspiration.

Miller's mural for the club was called "Love Through the Ages." The title seems to promise erotic delights, but the elaborate result was tongue in cheek and cartoonish. Eleanor Jewett, reviewing it for the *Chicago Tribune*, felt it wasn't naughty enough.[15] Other artists contributed to the club as well. One corner featured a small mural depicting, in a quasi-medieval style, the four suits in a deck of cards, the work of William P. Welsh, who is best known for a prizewinning series of Art Deco posters he did for the Pullman Sleeping Car Company.

A third Chicago painter who contributed to the decor of the Tavern Club was John Warner Norton, the organization's second president. He was born into a wealthy family in Lockport, Illinois, in 1876. Although his name is nearly unknown today, he was famous in the Jazz Age. When he died in 1934, Robert Harshe, director of the Art Institute of Chicago, said, "John was the preeminent personality in the art of the Midwest." Notable murals of his in the Windy City include those done for the Cliff Dwellers Club (1909–1910), Fuller Park Assembly Hall (1913–1914), Peirce School (1924–1925), the Daily News Building (1929; see chapter 8), the Chicago Board of Trade Building (1930; see chapter 15), and the Elizabeth M. Cudahy Memorial Library at Loyola University (1930).[16] He was also an instructor at the School of the Art Institute of Chicago, where his students included John Steuart Curry and Archibald Motley Jr., America's preeminent African American artist. When a retrospective of Norton's work was mounted in Chicago in 1992, *Chicago Tribune* art critic Alan G. Artner wrote, "Unlike a number of recent exhibitions that claimed to have rediscovered important Chicago or Illinois artists, the John Warner Norton show . . . really is a rediscovery and the artist is really important. . . . His initial achievement was to introduce American subject matter and reinterpret traditional symbols in a new 'modern' light."[17]

Opposite: In the early twenty-first century, the Michigan Avenue entrance of 333 North Michigan was restored, complete with Art Deco replacement sconces that were not exact copies of the originals but might be even more attractive. Photograph by Andrea Blatz.

Norton's murals covered three walls of the Tavern Club's west solarium, an avant-garde "moderne" chamber described as "cubistic in design and vivid in colors."[18] One of the most famous (or notorious) panels was a leafy scene depicting what seemed to be a seated philosopher accompanied by an undressed nymph or sprite. Norton never gave it a name, but over the years "Pagan Paradise" caught on. In the spring of 1930, the Tavern Club put on a show at the Goodman Theatre called "April Fooleries." The extravaganza included music and skits (one involving the poet Carl Sandburg, a member), and for a grand finale the members staged a live recreation of "Pagan Paradise" accompanied by music. Reporter Bill Welsh wrote, "We duplicated that painting exactly, with a real live nymph and philosopher. Yes, sir, we had a real nymph just the way she is in the painting without a stitch of clothes on. And she was beautiful! Looked as if she had just stepped down from a Grecian urn. Her name was Trudye."[19]

The tower was so impressive it inspired poetry. The ode "333," by poet and novelist Amy F. Greif, appeared in *The Chicagoan* in March 1930:

They say that once the red-man stood and gazed
Across the prairie, where this far-flung street
Makes echoes with the march of many feet;
That here, the buffalo at evening grazed,
Where now white topless towers are proudly
  raised,
Proclaiming man's achievement—shaft and spire
And stately obelisk catch morning's fire,
And in their mirrored windows sunsets blaze.
Yet one alone among them stands—alone and free,
Set just enough apart, alone to say,
"Let my white beauty dominate and see
How other aspirations fall away."
And so the slender grace we call "333,"
Built for the ages, smiles at man's short-lived day.

Prominent Chicago artist John Warner Norton painted several murals for the Tavern Club at 333 North Michigan. This panel, nicknamed "Pagan Paradise," made quite a stir when club members recreated it live, complete with nude model. 333 North Michigan Avenue, Tavern Club, Chicago, Illinois. Holabird and Root, architects. Historic Architecture and Landscape Image Collection, Ryerson and Burnham Art and Architecture Archives, The Art Institute of Chicago. Digital File # 37603.

Hampton Inn
Hampton Inn

No. 2

CHICAGO MOTOR CLUB

HOLABIRD & ROOT, 1929

This graceful gray fifteen-story limestone spire displays probably the most dramatic verticality of any Art Deco skyscraper in Chicago. As discussed in the introduction, in 1923 the city enacted an ordinance that permitted supertall skyscrapers if their profiles were set back in stages as they rose. The Chicago Motor Club building, because its base was only 48 feet wide and its height, at 260 feet, was 4 feet below the height limit, was not subject to this rule. It therefore springs straight up from the sidewalk to the sky. It's located at 68 E. Wacker Place, which is not a major thoroughfare and doesn't get the foot traffic that a building on, say, Michigan Avenue does, so it's hardly one of the better-known skyscrapers in Chicago. But it's a wonder, not only for its verticality but also for its Art Deco ornamentation.

Two days before the opening of the building on January 28, 1929, H. M. Brown, general manager of the club, said it was "the first office building in Chicago to embody the 'art moderne' theme."[1] Not quite, because 333 North Michigan preceded it, but he was close enough, and the statement shows how executives had become aware of the new style and had begun to champion it.

Advertisement for "The New Home of the Chicago Motor Club." Author's collection.

In the Jazz Age automobiles were hardly new but they were becoming omnipresent. In 1920 the number of car registrations in Chicago was ninety thousand; in 1930 it was nearly half a million. By 1929, when the Chicago Motor Club building opened, yearly American automobile production had reached 5.3 million. In a single decade, the automobile transformed American life. Art Deco and the automobile age arrived together, and this building symbolizes their compatibility.

Cars weren't new, but traveling by car was still something of a novelty. Vacationers were discovering the freedom of the great American road trip. Miles of roads were being paved, and facilities like the auto court (a collection of tiny cabins) would eventually transform into motels, while gas stations and diners proliferated. Hundreds of those gas stations and diners were built in the Art Deco style, and for Americans who never visited big cities, the highways became showcases of Art Deco. Even travelers who didn't go by car experienced the style by boarding at Greyhound bus stations, which were themselves often displays of streamlining.[2]

Although bus drivers knew where they were going, motorists found that roads were often unmarked, and it was easy to get lost. The numbering of US highways and the standardization of road signs, which introduced different shapes for Stop signs, Yield signs, Railroad Crossing signs, and so on, did not begin until the late 1920s. Drivers needed help. And the Chicago Motor Club came to their rescue.

In the first years of the twentieth century, automobiles were expensive and mostly playthings of the wealthy, a situation that made early automobile clubs a kind of social gathering place for a bunch of rich guys (about fifty such clubs operated nationally in the first decade of the century). The Chicago Motor Club, founded in 1906, set out to be different. It lobbied governments for better roads, street widening, the rerouting of streetcars, and safety features such as traffic lights and mandated headlights. The club was especially active in an initiative called "The Fight for Good Roads."

The club had its first headquarters, naturally, on Chicago's Motor Row—a South Michigan Avenue strip between 14th and 24th Streets where, at one time,

well over one hundred types of cars were displayed and sold (today it's a historic district). In 1915 the Chicago Motor Club became a chapter of the American Automobile Association (AAA) but remained careful to retain its own identity. The club successively occupied four sites on Motor Row, but when the membership grew to seventy thousand the directors realized the need for a large modern building—if not on Motor Row at least near Michigan Avenue.

Motorists crowd into the lobby of the Chicago Motor Club for travel information. Chicago Motor Club Building, Chicago, Illinois. Holabird and Root, architects. Historic Architecture and Landscape Image Collection, Ryerson and Burnham Art and Architecture Archives, The Art Institute of Chicago. Digital File # 44236.

In a newspaper ad for their new headquarters, the club claimed that "prominent architects agree this is the most beautiful building in America." It certainly has a dramatic entryway, in which three doors are

Stylized map of the United States by John Warner Norton. Photograph by Andrea Blatz.

enclosed in a cast iron frame, with supertall windows above—openings that allow abundant light to flow into the three-story lobby, which the Commission on Chicago Landmarks has called "one of the finest Art Deco interior spaces in Chicago."

On the east side of the stylish lobby, a motorist could get maps as well as hotel information and, beginning in 1937, an itinerary by means of a personal TripTik, a five-inch-wide book that showed not only routes but also tourist sights, places to eat, and lodging. A club newspaper advertisement from the period read, "If a Chicago Motor Club member, our Touring Bureau will supply you, free of charge, complete routing—logs and maps showing detours, dangerous crossings, etc.—all the latest information from our numerous correspondents." Although Prohibition was in effect when the club opened, it was said that a motorist in the know could procure a glass of "giggle water" from the bar.

On the west side of the lobby is a bank of three elevators (originally Otis Signal Control Elevators). Above them is a giant pastel-colored mural of a map of the United States by the artist and muralist John Warner Norton (see chapter 1.) Norton's biographer, Jim L. Zimmer, has written of this map, "The stylized cartographic image in cool and warm grays, light greens, orange-reds, and warm tans highlights the country's principal cities, national parks, and national highways. Norton wisely used a series of geometric motifs to symbolize mountain ranges, parks, and bodies of water."[3]

As the Commission on Chicago Landmarks describes the Chicago Motor Club, "the building is elaborately detailed with a plethora of Art Deco-style ornament, including stylized flowers and plants, flowing fountains of water, zigzags, swirls and sunbursts." The facade of the 89,000-square-foot building is divided into three vertical sections, the middle being a protruding semicircular bay. The tall cast iron frame of the entrance is the building's most dramatic feature. Above the doors are Native American feather motifs.

The tower sits on a double-decker street, so the entryway is technically on the second floor. The base of the front is granite, and the tower is Indiana limestone, although face brick is used on the three less visible sides. In the central bay the windows are separated by decorative terra-cotta spandrels using Art Deco motifs of flowers, birds, and geometric forms. Most of the exterior ornamental work is done in metal. In addition to the map mural, the interior features abundant decoration, some in nickel alloy, the material also used for the railings on the spiral staircase, which has marble steps.

In the 1980s the Chicago Motor Club moved to suburban Des Plaines. The building didn't close, however, and served as rental space for various businesses under the name Wacker Tower. Unfortunately, by 2004 demolition loomed. There was talk—as there was throughout Chicago and other American cities by that time—about recycling older buildings as condominiums. Plans to do that with the Chicago Motor Club building were made. Each apartment would occupy an entire floor, which meant windows on four sides. The developer also planned to install balconies on the west side. Condo prices started at $1.4 million and went up to nearly $4 million. Sales were disappointing, in part because the devastating 2008 recession had arrived.

In 2011 the building was put up for court-ordered auction. The suggested opening bid: $500,000—less than a one-family house in many Windy City neighborhoods. That proposal was likely something of a publicity stunt; real estate gurus at the time figured it would go for ten times that, and in fact two years later *Crain's* reported that it had sold for $9.5 million to developers planning to turn it into a 144-room hotel. One of the factors preventing its demolition was the size of the lot; developers were not that interested in squeezing a replacement tower into such a small space. After a decade of intense lobbying efforts by the Chicago Art Deco Society and the preservation group Landmarks Illinois, the Chicago Motor Club building gained landmark status in 2012, a designation that helped keep the building from being torn down.

A rescuer ultimately arrived in the form of developer John T. Murphy, president of Murphy Asset Management, who engineered a $41 million makeover of the skyscraper into a Hampton Inn hotel. The job

Art Deco decorations on the exterior of the Chicago Motor Club. Photograph by the author.

of renovation was given to a team from Hartshorne Plunkard Architecture headed by architect Paul Allesandro, who described the challenges. "What remained of the original exuberant design had been replaced," he wrote, "by a dull sameness and stagnation that masked the original sense of enthusiasm and movement."[4] The original colors of the lobby were restored and Art Deco light fixtures, lying forgotten in a rooftop chamber, were reinstalled. The removal of white granite tiles revealed the original terrazzo floor. The spiral staircase was rejuvenated, and the exterior masonry was cleaned. The original entrance canopy, however, was long gone, necessitating the design and construction of a new one. "We discovered that the walls in the lobby area had been painted over many times," Alessandro explained. "We quickly noticed that the mural was really a part of the architecture and that the lobby area's color scheme was initially the same as that of the mural. Thus the original paint scheme on the lobby walls was restored, as was the plaster ornamentation, much of which is silver leafed, revealing a nature motif with leaves, birds, and geometric patterns."

When the hotel opened, Blair Kamin, architecture critic for the *Chicago Tribune*, exulted, "Thank goodness such irreplaceable visual richness is still with us."[5] The Chicago Motor Club is an emblem of Art Deco, but it is also an example of the right way to recycle an older building.

RENTALS
(312) 944•5700
ONLY

No. 3

10 WEST ELM

B. LEO STEIF, 1929

In early 1928, Philip Hampson of the *Chicago Tribune* cheerfully announced, "City to Have Gay Colored Skyscraper."[1] He went on to explain that Samuel Cole, president of the 10 West Elm Street Building corporation, had engaged architect B. Leo Steif to design a "nineteen story apartment and exclusive shop building" at the northwest corner of State and Elm Streets. "The first floor is to be of dark French blue terra cotta. The second, third, and fourth floors will be a light blue green, almost a robin's egg blue, terra cotta. Then the mass of the structure will be a salmon colored face brick. And the five upper floors will be trimmed in a multi-colored terra cotta composed of five hues. Crowning the structure will be a mansard of copper which ultimately will be a rich green through process of oxidation."

This rainbow was possible through the use of terra-cotta, which means "baked earth." It's an unglazed ceramic that has been used globally for over two thousand years and can be made in many colors. In architecture it's necessary to distinguish two kinds of terra-cotta: architectural and structural. Architectural terra-cotta is used for cornices, sills, lintels, and

As one of the finest examples of terra-cotta in the city, 10 West Elm was featured in an advertisement by the Northwestern Terra Cotta Company of Chicago. Author's collection.

other features that are commonly decorated. Structural terra-cotta is used for walls, arches, partitions, and as wrapping on steel columns to fireproof them, which partly explains its desirable qualities. In 1920, Charles E. White Jr., a terra-cotta expert, explained that the material is "durable, beautiful, and economical . . . Properly made terra cotta is fire-resistant, frost-proof, and weather-proof, in which characteristics it is superior to stone. It lends itself to a great variety of color effects and can be molded or ornamented with comparative ease to produce either plain or intricately ornamented work that will stand the wear and tear of centuries."[2] Another advantage of terra-cotta is that it can be scrubbed clean. As a 1930 advertisement from the National Terra Cotta Society said, "All architectural material can be cleaned to the extent that some part of the accumulated grime can be removed. But only in Terra Cotta can the original color and freshness of surface be fully restored."

Terra-cotta itself can't support great weights, but when Chicago architects invented the curtain wall for skyscrapers it became, in the words of 1920s builder William Starrett, "structurally feasible," since most of the weight was carried elsewhere. (The "curtain wall" was another name for the iron framework of girders that supported tall buildings. The innovation meant walls no longer needed to be load-bearing because they hung on the framework like a curtain.) Starrett went on to say, "Lighter than stone or brick, highly fire resistant and sturdy . . . it is also very cheap and capable of infinite ornamentation, coloration and imitation of more expensive materials."[3] In Starrett's opinion, however, architects were tempted to overuse it, slapping on "cartouches" and "festoons of abundance and cornucopias" in a style he caricatured as "Early Pullman Car," by which he meant overdecorated in an ostentatious Victorian manner. That mania dwindled, however, when architects realized that although the material was cheap, the labor costs were not: "Such geegaws were expensive in labor if not in material, and the pruning hook began to trim them ruthlessly from the tree of architecture."

According to Jean L. Guarino, "Chicago was the epicenter of the terracotta industry, the popularity of which peaked in the 1920s."[4] Indeed, three of the main manufacturers in the country were headquartered in Chicago—the American Terra Cotta & Ceramics Co., the Midland Terra Cotta Co., and the Northwestern Terra Cotta Co., the largest in the United States. Northwestern made terra-cotta ornamentation for the Civic Opera House (see chapter 9), the Chicago Theatre, the Wrigley Building, and Randolph Tower and did a lot of work for Frank Lloyd Wright.[5] Other famous Chicago skyscrapers that use terra-cotta include the Marquette Building, the Carbide and Carbon Building (see chapter 6), and the Reliance Building, which Starrett says was the first to do so. But terra-cotta can be found in more than 2,500 Chicago buildings, many of which are smaller structures—theaters, auto repair shops, stores, and so on. Most builders ordered terra-cotta ornamentation from a company's stock catalog.

Some of the city's most lavish terra-cotta is on the Laramie State Bank on West Chicago Avenue in the Austin neighborhood, one of the Northwestern Terra Cotta Company's finest achievements and one of Chicago's greatest Art Deco structures. But before being put on the National Register of Historic Places in 2023, it was considered one of the city's most endangered buildings. The structure was almost falling apart, which brings up a problem with terra-cotta. The stuff is practically indestructible, but it needs upkeep. One author compared terra-cotta to teeth—they're both tough, durable enamel, but without routine care bad things can happen. One of the biggest threats to architectural terra-cotta is the freeze-thaw cycle that corrodes the anchors that fasten it to a building's walls. In 1999 a Chicago woman walking along Michigan Avenue was struck by a terra-cotta fragment falling from the Art Deco Carbide and Carbon Building. She was taken to the hospital and released without serious injury. The newspaper story stated that similar occurrences had recently happened with the facades of other Chicago terra-cotta structures, so "the city has formed a task force to inspect all 245 terra cotta-clad buildings in the downtown area."[6] When the Carbide and Carbon Building was restored in the early twenty-first century, 7,700 terra-cotta blocks had to be replaced.

The terra-cotta used on the "gay colored skyscraper," now known as 10 West Elm, was another achievement by Northwestern Terra Cotta Co. The panels were the work of sculptor Edouard Chassaing, who was born in Clermont-Ferrand, France, in 1895 and came to the United States with his wife, Olga, who was also a sculptor. He was one of six sculptors brought in from France by Northwestern after the celebrated 1925 Art Deco exhibition in Paris. Various of his works can be found around Chicago (an attractive Madonna and Child is in St. Thomas the Apostle Church in Hyde Park). His most formidable sculpture is the statue called *Hope and Help* (1955), depicting a surgeon lifting a suffering man, that stands in front

of the International Museum of Surgical Science on North Lake Shore Drive.

Benjamin Leo Steif, the building's architect, was just thirty-four and making his name in the Windy City. He was born in New York City but came to Illinois as a youth and attended first the University of Illinois and then the Armour Institute (today the Illinois Institute of Technology), from which he graduated in 1916. Before 10 West Elm, he designed a women's clothing shop on Michigan Avenue done in the style of Louis XV, a three-story apartment and retail building (now demolished) on North Milwaukee Avenue in the Logan Square neighborhood, and an elegant Tudor Gothic apartment tower at 3800 North Lake Shore Drive, which still stands. These buildings gave no hint of Art Deco, and when the 10 West Elm edifice was first announced in 1927, the *Chicago Tribune* reported the building was designed in a "German renaissance style with all the exterior walls of the same material," which is practically the opposite of how it turned out.[7] Clearly, Steif adopted the new Art Deco aesthetic when he described 10 West Elm as "the latest idea of modern French design," which was how it was advertised. Why the change? Steif visited New York City, where he made sketches of two recent buildings, the Insurance Center and the Savoy-Plaza Hotel. As architectural historian John Zukowsky explains, "The chateau roof and polychrome brick and masonry of the Savoy Plaza are akin to a similarly massed roof and polychrome terracotta and brick in Steif's project. Although his sketch is undated, it is probable that these buildings, especially the Savoy Plaza, influenced the design of Steif's apartment tower."[8]

This spread: Terra-cotta roof details on 10 West Elm. Photographs by Ian McClellan.

The plan of 10 West Elm demonstrates an alternative to the "Grand Art Deco formula" of a granite base supporting a limestone tower. The *AIA Guide to Chicago* remarks, "In contrast to the magisterial streamlining of Holabird & Root and Graham, Anderson, Probst & White, here is the brash side of the late 1920s."[9] Steif explained to *Tribune* reporter Hampson "that the city's narrow streets make it difficult to give the skyscraper its full due in design and that he is using colors in the State and Elm structure to enhance the architectural effects—the colors producing the illusion of shadows, etc."[10] The apartments were not large (each had two to five rooms), and architectural historian Neil Harris speculates that the exterior on this and other "colorfully decorated residential hotels and inexpensive apartment complexes . . . are more inventive, modernistic, and ornamentally memorable than their more expensive and expansive counterparts. Indeed, it could be argued that designers of some of the more modest interiors overcompensated in their efforts to command attention."[11]

Observers of the architectural scene in 1920s Chicago disapproved of what they called "rooftop atrocities"—water tanks and elevator machinery—and advised hiding such eyesores behind parapets, towers, and other such devices, as Steif did at 10 West Elm with the aforementioned "mansard of copper." In another nod to restraint, Steif said "he is not going to have the building cluttered up with a lot of signs; the shops on the lower floors will have to get along without them."[12] Even before the tower was completed, the Michigan Avenue–based The French Shops, purveyors of antiques and furniture, signed a lease for the second and third floors and part of the first. This was a clear sign that the building was considered to be in a desirable location. And so it remains.

HOT MULLIGAN

No. 4

NORTHWEST TOWER

PERKINS, CHATTEN & HAMMOND, 1929

"The Skyscraper Leaves the Loop."

That was the headline in *The Greater Chicago Magazine* in February 1929. Towers were sprouting throughout Chicago's downtown, but this was different. The article went on: "Here, in this famous old neighborhood, one of the most populous areas in the city, known as the Wicker Park District, this handsome edifice dominates the scene, and takes rank at once as the outstanding landmark of the great northwest side."[1]

Located about four miles northwest of downtown, the Northwest Tower (the magazine preferred "North West Tower") was in an uncommon place for a skyscraper, but the neighborhood was bustling and well able to support such a large structure. *The Greater Chicago Magazine* reported the area was "the second largest retail district in the city."

Today, the area has been landmarked as the "Milwaukee Avenue District." According to the Commission on Chicago Landmarks, it "retains a solid and exceptional group of historic neighborhood commercial buildings, with a broad range of architectural styles from the late-nineteenth through the early-twentieth

One of the most noteworthy aspects of the Northwest Tower was its location—away from downtown, as seen in the February 1929 issue of *The Greater Chicago Magazine*. Chicago History Museum, ICHi-18909.

centuries. . . . The resulting rich mix of building types and styles gives the district a visually distinct and urban character within the neighborhood context of Chicago's Northwest Side."

The neighborhood took off after the Great Chicago Fire of 1871. That conflagration left Wicker Park untouched, so many survivors relocated to affordable housing there. After the fire, Chicago's elites sought to establish a building code that permitted only fireproof masonry buildings, but the working classes protested that this measure would put the cost of a new home out of their reach. A compromise was reached in that the central commercial districts would require masonry but districts farther out would continue to

The spire of the Northwest Tower is decorated with Art Deco–styled medieval knights. Photograph by the author.

allow wooden houses—and Milwaukee Avenue was designated one of those timber-friendly zones.

In the first post-fire decades, the ethnic composition of the neighborhood was mostly German and Scandinavian, but it shifted to predominantly Polish—so much so that the area became known as the capital of "Polonia," and the plaza at the intersection of Ashland, Division, and Milwaukee is known as the "Polonia Triangle" or "Polish Triangle." Many Polish immigrants came to Chicago because the fire had created a labor shortage.[2] In 1929, when the Northwest Tower opened, Wicker Park was 64 percent Polish, 10 percent Russian, 8 percent German, 8 percent American, and 4 percent Austrian.[3]

In 1895, Chicago's elevated transit system (the famous "L") had reached the neighborhood, which now made it part of the urban grid. The train runs just a block south of the Northwest Tower, and streetcars also ran on Robey (now Damen) and North Avenues. Banks, theaters, light industry, and department stores prospered. In 1912 the *Chicago Tribune* commented, "Milwaukee Avenue, one of the more interesting streets in Chicago, for many reasons has . . . experienced a boom in values, which in some of the more favored parts has been of a sensational character."[4] Because the street was thriving, the need for office space grew.

In 1905 a businessman named Joseph R. Noel opened, in the face of considerable skepticism, a bank in Wicker Park, where he saw a potential that others missed ("density of population" and "unexcelled transportation facilities," for starters). He believed that "opportunities constantly surround us, like the air we breathe, few of us being able to see them any more than we can see the air."[5] In 1919 his Noel State Bank purchased for $110,000 a 134-by-138-foot lot on a corner of the six-cornered junction of Milwaukee, Damen, and North Avenues. A busy intersection, it is sometimes inelegantly called "the Crotch." The origin of the nickname is unclear; some have speculated that it has to do with the shape of the intersection, the traffic snarls, or that it can get odiferous on a busy Saturday night.

The construction firm E. F. Wilson & Co. built the Northwest Tower in about nine months, from a design by the firm of Perkins, Chatten & Hammond. It was reported that Mr. Wilson "personally supervised the construction . . . and gave personal attention to the subcontractors under his direction."[6] Perkins, Chatten & Hammond was formed in early 1927 when Dwight H. Perkins left his decades-long association with Perkins, Fellows & Hamilton, which specialized in school and college design, and teamed up with Melville C. Chatten and C. Herrick Hammond. The skyscraper they designed for Noel follows the "Grand Art Deco formula" of a granite base supporting an Indiana limestone tower. The facade is cleverly varied by alternating piers and window spandrels.

The elevators in the Northwest Tower, made by the Westinghouse Electric Elevator Company, employed an innovation called "Variable Voltage" and were the most up to date in the city. Photograph by the author.

The building is twelve stories tall, which is not a lot for a Chicago skyscraper, but its location makes a difference. As Al Chase, real estate editor at the *Chicago Tribune*, said at the time, "a twelve story building in that district of low buildings will loom on the horizon even more conspicuously than a forty story tower in the much towered loop." And so it looms today, as no competing towers have been erected since (the Great Depression put the skyscraper era on a two-decade hiatus). The tower might have even been taller, but its twelve stories were the maximum allowed by the zoning laws for the area. Chase also remarked: "In one particular the new Northwest Tower puts to shame some of our newest and practically all of our old time skyscrapers in the loop. It has no unsightly zigzag of sprawling fire escapes disfiguring the architectural lines of the structure. Following the example of Tribune Tower these are concealed in fire towers inside the building, for which the neighboring property owners and dwellers should give Joseph R. Noel, chairman of the board of directors of the Noel State Bank, a rising vote of thanks."[7]

The builders promoted the new tower as being up to date: "Everything is characterized by a noiseless efficiency throughout the building. Two high speed new type elevators, equipped with the latest automatic levelling devices, afford excellent service to the building and remove all need for 'step up' or 'step down, please.' The danger of stumbling is non-existent. In place of the old-fashioned unsightly outside fire escapes, the North West Tower is provided with an enclosed fire-shield stairway which ensures increased safety for the building's occupants. . . . Heating is by vacuum steam radiation from oil-burning boilers, with a resulting absence of all dust and noise usual in coal deliveries."[8] The elevators were installed by the Westinghouse Electric Elevator Company and employed a company innovation called "Variable Voltage," which ensured smooth operation. Fortunately, the original elevators, with their classic Art Deco bronze doors, are still in place. And as Chase noted at the time, many of the upper floors were occupied by doctors and dentists, with appropriate utility connections.

A promotional card depicting the sparkling Northwest Tower when it was brand new. Author's collection.

Like several other skyscrapers of the era, the tower sports a cupola, or spire, sheathed in bronze, but here the spire was placed not in the center of the building but at the most prominent corner. Originally, it was illuminated by floodlights ("a beacon for the entire district," according to *The Greater Chicago Magazine*) and was open to the public, who were pleased to discover that could see Lake Michigan from the spire. Some observers said the spire suggested the upturned head of a wolf or coyote howling at the moon, and the building was later given the nickname "Coyote Building." From 1989 until 2010, an "Around the Coyote" community arts festival, to support emerging artists not only in the Wicker Park community but also internationally, was held in dozens of area buildings.

By that time, the neighborhood had become hip and revitalized. Not so the Coyote Building itself, which was clad in scaffolding and half vacant. A local developer, Krzysztof Karbowski, bought the tower for $5 million in 2007 and hatched a plan to develop it as a hotel, but the venture fell through because of financing problems mostly caused by the Great Recession of 2008. Although the neighborhood had become rejuvenated, it was unclear what function such a large building might serve. In 2012, however, Chicago-based DRW Real Estate Investments acquired the tower and chose Grupo Habita, based in Mexico City, to transform it into a boutique hotel and oversee renovations. The architectural firm Antunovich Associates repaired the spandrels and limestone panels, while putting in new windows that reproduced the originals, and Belgian architects Nicolas Schuybroek and Marc Merckx Interiors restored the terrazzo, brass, and marble lobby, which still had the original brass elevator doors and elevator floor indicators. The large windows at the base of the tower became attractive interfaces of a new corner restaurant named Cafe Robey. The cupola received new glass and a flag. The tower thus became one of the latest historic Chicago commercial structures to be transformed into hotels—alongside the Reliance Building, the Chicago Athletic Association, the London Guarantee & Accident Building, the Old Dearborn Bank Building, the Chicago Motor Club, and the Carbide and Carbon Building.

№. 5

POWHATAN APARTMENTS

ROBERT DEGOLYER & CHARLES L. MORGAN, 1929

From a contemporary perspective, apartment buildings are quintessential symbols of the modern era and of urban life. But they are nothing new; the ancient Romans, for example, had multistory structures called *insulae*. Yet the *insulae*, like other historical apartment buildings, were for plebians; wealthy Romans resided in villas.

By the late nineteenth century, however, apartment life had changed. The rich were persuaded that it was not low-class to live in an apartment house. In fact, changing conditions made it almost necessary. Writing in *Architectural Forum* in 1930, Electus D. Litchfield explained,

> There are still those who prefer the luxury and prestige, even coupled with the attendant troubles, of the private house; but taxes and servant troubles have become so much of a burden that . . . the private house bids fair to soon become extinct. Everyone knows that the wages of domestic servants have increased tremendously since the war, and the great difficulty there is in obtaining well trained and adequate servants. Gone are

> those paragons who served in our mothers' homes. The invention of labor-saving devices for cleaning, cooking and for the laundry have seemed to reduce, rather than to increase, what the average maid considers a full day's work. Less space and less waste space in the home seems a necessity.[1]

Litchfield went on to describe how, one by one, the opulent New York single-family manors of the rich had been replaced by large apartment houses. It was a process being repeated in Chicago. In the Gold Coast, one could still find "the imposing stone mansions, with their green lawns and wrought-iron-grilled doorways, of Chicago's wealthy aristocracy and industrial and financial kings," but just to the south, in the neighborhood known as Streeterville, stood posh new apartment houses, where rents ran as high as $1,000 a month ($15,000 in today's money).[2] Soon, well-appointed apartment blocks replaced nearly all the great houses on Lake Shore Drive, too. A turning point came when an entrepreneur named Clinton J. Warren began to understand that apartment buildings had to look different from hotels and devised ways, such as courtyard apartments and luxury elevators, to set them apart.[3]

In 1922, 18,125 apartment units were built in Chicago. Within five years, the figure reached a new high of 36,875. The Chicago Zoning Commission counted 750,000 people living in single-family houses and 2 million in apartment buildings.[4] (The effect of the Great Depression was so ruinous that by 1933 the number of new units had dwindled to 21.)[5] The figures for the nation were similar. According to the *Architectural Record*, in 1929, "Throughout all cities over 100,000, of which there are 85 . . . we have built 60% multifamily as against 40% single-family houses."[6]

In 1928 the Chicago real estate firm Baird & Warner published *A Portfolio of Fine Apartment Homes*, a twelve-by-nineteen-inch illustrated volume with listings of ninety-three luxurious apartment buildings, many taller than the "canonic" twelve stories, that ran north on, or near, the lakeshore from the Chicago River to, and including, Evanston. (The book excluded many fine buildings on the southern lakefront.) Twenty-six of the buildings were fifteen stories or higher—the tallest being the thirty-story Drake Tower at 179 East Lake Shore Drive—and the apartments ranged in size from one room to eighteen.[7] A writer in *The Chicagoan* commented in 1929 that twenty years previously, "the little gray home in Chicago had a light in the window and a child waiting at the gate; now it has an electric sign on the roof and a uniformed attendant at the door."[8]

By the late 1920s, the trendy topic in the real estate business was not apartment buildings per se, but cooperative apartment buildings, a relatively new concept. In Chicago most of these co-ops were constructed along the lakefront. They were large and comfortable but within the price range of upper-middle-class buyers who now had a sensible alternative to financing a single-family home or paying rent to a landlord. But co-ops also appealed to the wealthy, who leased some magnificent units. In 1919 there was not a single co-op building in Chicago, in 1920 there were two, and in 1930 there were one hundred.[9]

A co-op is an apartment building that's owned not by a single landlord, but by a corporation. Buyers do not purchase an apartment; they purchase a share of the corporation, which includes a permanent lease on the apartment, held not only by the owner but also by the owner's heirs. Buyers thereby become shareholders. Co-ops are regulated by bylaws and a board of directors, and maintenance is financed by monthly fees paid by the shareholders.

In 1927 the *Chicago Tribune* published an investigative piece, "Is There a 'Joker' in the Co-op Apartment Proposition?"[10] The author, Harry A. Rick, asked, "Have the thousands of owners who have put more than $125,000,000 in co-operative apartments in Chicago been 'stung'? Or have they—*as they think*—made a sound investment and found a solution to the high cost of maintaining a home?" Early co-ops, Rick noted, tended to be shaky propositions, but after official real estate boards established co-op departments, there had been "great improvement." These departments, he explained, were established "for the purpose of squelching unscrupulous co-operative projects and to supply information and comparative statistics relative to the financing, building, sale and operation of co-operative properties." Rick concluded that co-op life was less expensive than home ownership. "How these savings are accomplished," he explained, "is obvious to anyone who can see that one lot, one heating plant, one plumbing system, one roof, one architect's fee, one legal fee, one building profit, etc., for fifty or one hundred families cost vastly less than fifty or a hundred such items that must go into the cost of any building, large or small."

One of the key benefits of a co-op, Rick pointed out, is that it "enables you to hand-pick your neighbors"—that is, to live with people of whom you approve. The co-op "can be a powerful agency for controlling the caste of the entire neighborhood," he said. Rick concluded by naming some of the rich and famous who had chosen co-op living, names that still resonate today: Charles Evans Hughes and Elihu Root (both former secretaries of state), Mrs. William Vanderbilt, Percy Rockefeller, Henry F. du Pont, John G. Shedd, and others.

Co-ops especially interested the writer Ruth G. Bergman at *The Chicagoan*, who published several articles on the phenomenon, mostly favorable. "While the co-operative owner is rarely the builder," she said, "he demands good construction when he buys and usually gets it.... Furthermore, when a man buys he is generally willing to pay for luxuries which he would forego on a monthly rental basis. Thus co-ops run to genuine walnut paneling, filtered water in every apartment, tiled walls in every bath and kitchen."[11] "Co-operative apartment building is in its infancy," she observed, "but what a big, bouncing, assertive infant it is."[12]

An article in *Architectural Forum* in 1930 complained of the meretricious design of many apartment houses, in which the builders mistakenly thought "that the exterior and interior characteristics of the one-family dwelling should be incorporated in the apartment building." But the author hoped that the plans of co-ops would lead to improvement: "The cooperative apartment building is a radical development in that the occupants are owners instead of tenants. An owner is more interested in the quality of the home than is a tenant and, perhaps, possesses more discrimination and knowledge.... The cooperative apartment building, because of its increasing excellence, may force an improvement in the architectural design of the tenant-occupied apartment building."[13]

That hoped-for change had already occurred in Chicago. Toward the end of 1927, Bergman reported, "A co-operative soon to be built on the old Chicago Beach properties promises a ballroom and a swimming pool; in fact, all the luxuries of an ocean liner."[14] This cooperative turned out to be the twenty-two-story Powhatan on South Chicago Beach Drive in Hyde Park. It was, and remains, the most desirable and stylish Art Deco cooperative apartment building in Chicago (and it does have both a swimming pool and a ballroom).

In the early 1920s, the area east of the Chicago Beach Hotel, a luxury resort built for Chicago's 1893 World's Columbian Exposition, was being expanded through landfill. Developers were eyeing the area as a South Side counterpart to Streeterville, which had also been built on landfill. A bond trader named Elzy Anderson Garard arranged the financing, and when construction began on the Powhatan in October 1928, half the units had already been sold.[15] The name of the building comes from the American Indian leader Powhatan, father of Pocahontas. Something of a fashion at the time for Indian-derived names also led to the naming of other nearby buildings, including The Narragansett, the Algonquin Apartments, and the Chippewa, and the designation of the area as Indian Village, as it is still called. As noted in the introduction, two aims of the Art Deco architectural movement in the United States were to be modern and to be American. And what could be more American than the American Indian? Philip Hampson, writing in the *Tribune* in 1927, was therefore pleased to report that the building, "will be especially interesting since it will be thoroughly American in its exterior design and in its interior decorative treatment... [it] will be characterized by the sweeping lines of the most up to the minute thought in American architecture.... Chief Powhatan's handsome features are going to appear throughout the structure in the form of bas reliefs. And the vivid coloring the Indians liked will be used in the ballroom and other community rooms. The lobby, too, will be decorated in a style reminiscent of Indian taste."[16]

Perhaps the first word that comes to mind when viewing the Powhatan from the street is "imposing." Verticality is an attribute of many Chicago Art Deco skyscrapers, but few emphasize it so forcefully. The narrow vertical rows of windows that spring upward in dark bands don't stop at the roof but extend into a parapet of pointed spires. At the top of the building is the ballroom, which has terraces with views of the city and the lake.

The architects were Robert DeGolyer and Charles L. Morgan. DeGolyer had wide experience designing apartment buildings in traditional, historical styles; the adoption of Art Deco showed that, at age fifty-two, he wasn't too old to learn new tricks, although he mostly concentrated on the engineering aspects of the Powhatan. Morgan, who was an unusual combination of artist, architect, and entrepreneur, was responsible for the design features, especially the decorations in and on the building. A graduate of the University of Illinois, he became an associate architect in Frank Lloyd Wright's firm and helped prepare drawings for Wright's ambitious, but unbuilt, National Life Insurance Building. Morgan formed a company called Mosaic Overmantels, which offered decorative mosaic pieces for interior decoration. He claimed to have four hundred colors in his repertory, which might be true because color abounds on the Powhatan's facade. The impressionistic treatment of Native American motifs and themes in Morgan's spandrels gives the Powhatan a multihued aspect not common on limestone skyscrapers. The shiny black spandrels on the second and third floors display more realistic representation of Native Americans and wildlife, while the entry doors bear more stylized representations. Morgan also created the tiles in the inner and outer lobbies, the swimming pool, and the ballroom. Assisting Morgan with

This spread: American Indian themes are to be found throughout the Powhatan, as on lights by the Chicago-based Victor S. Pearlman Co., which use Indian symbols with an Art Deco touch; in the exterior relief of an Indian chief; and on the entry doors. Photographs by the author.

the decorative motifs was Margaret T. Fairman, a talented Chicago artist who had become his assistant in 1926. The panels in the room between the lobby and the pool are especially noteworthy because they are so similar to those that were in Midway Gardens, a huge, prominently decorated dining and dancing complex designed by Wright that opened in 1913 just a few miles away. The Midway Gardens were demolished in 1929, the very year the Powhatan was built, and it has been suggested that Morgan meant the tiles as an homage to his mentor.

The interior of the Powhatan displays some of the finest Art Deco stylings in Chicago. Not all the Morgan mosaics survive, but those that do, such as the eight panels in the oval outer lobby, are captivating, drawing on a variety of decorative sources—Arabian, Chi-

Above: The Art Deco fireplace in the lobby of the Powhatan bears an ingenious rebus about when to put coal on the fire. Photograph by David Schalliol.

Left: The oval outer lobby of the Powhatan displays eight mosaic panels by artist, architect, and entrepreneur Charles Morgan. This attractive scene shows a woman playing what appears to be a mandolin. Before working on the Powhatan, Morgan had been an associate architect in Frank Lloyd Wright's firm. Photograph by David Schalliol.

nese, classical Greek, and of course, Native American (a warrior with a bow and arrow). Although, as historian Teri J. Edelstein has pointed out, two of the female figures "sport up-to-the-minute hairstyles of the 1920s."[17] The inner lobby mosaics, which lean toward abstraction while depicting unusual birds, give the impression, as art historian Mary Lackritz Gray put it, of a "vividly colored tropical rain forest."[18] These were covered for decades and were rediscovered during a restoration in 1996–1997. On the fireplace in the inner lobby is a witty rebus that bears explaining. It reads "If the B mt put :/ If the B. putting:" and the key to deciphering it is to read "B" as "Great B (grate be)," "mt" as "empty," ":" as "colon (coal on)," and "." as "full

Exterior panels by Charles Morgan. Photograph by Ian McClellan.

stop." Thus: "If the grate be empty, put coal on / If the grate be full stop putting coal on." In many cases the Art Deco elevators, which still have their original paneling and brass doors using crane motifs, open into the units.[19]

Morgan drowned at a Florida resort in 1947 while trying to retrieve a ball kicked into a river by a group of children. His name might not be famous, but few other Chicago artists offer such a massive, permanent, outdoor display of their works.

DeGolyer, who died at age seventy-six in 1952 (peacefully, as far as we know), went on to be part of the team that designed the historic Julia C. Lathrop Homes in Chicago as well as one of the assistant architects on the Pentagon. His legacy, however, consists mostly of his elegant Windy City apartment buildings—1241 and 3750 Lake Shore Drive and the Marlborough Apartments, for example, in addition to the Powhatan. One of his apartment buildings—200 East Pearson—has an interesting story to tell. For years it was home to none other than Ludwig Mies van der Rohe, the champion of "less is more" modernism. It seems he preferred this most comfortable and elegant Italian-style palazzo to one of his own minimalist apartment buildings. As architectural historian Sally Kitt Chappell remarked, "Critics of modernism have enjoyed pointing out this irony ever since."[20]

No. 6

CARBIDE AND CARBON BUILDING

BURNHAM BROTHERS, 1929

"Green 'nd Gold Tower Newest for Boul Mich," declared the headline of a *Chicago Tribune* story on May 13, 1928. The piece went on to explain, "Although color is fast becoming an important factor in the sale of most American products, owners and architects have overlooked to a notable extent its use in buildings. The Carbide tower, however, will be an exception, for D.H. Burnham & Co. have designed a structure to be entirely in green and gold, with a black base. It will be 505 feet above sidewalk level."[1] The building's location on North Michigan Avenue was part of a trend initiated by the opening of the Michigan Avenue Bridge (now the DuSable Bridge) in 1920. Two other Art Deco skyscrapers—333 North Michigan and the Chicago Motor Club—are barely a block away.

The architects, Daniel Burnham Jr. and his brother Hubert, were the sons of the illustrious Chicago architect Daniel Burnham (1846–1912). They founded their own firm in 1917, originally giving it the name of their father's company, D. H. Burnham and Co., but they changed it to Burnham Brothers, Inc. in 1928. The brothers designed several important Chicago structures, including the Central Life Insurance Building

Opposite: The first four floors of the Carbide and Carbon Building are faced with shiny polished black granite. The upper floors are different shades of mottled green terra-cotta with attractive Art Deco flourishes. Photograph by Ian McClellan.

Above: The Wacker Place entrance of the Carbide and Carbon Building. Photograph by the author.

(1924), the Michael A. Bilandic Building (1924; a.k.a. the Burnham Building), the Seneca Hotel (1926), the Engineering Building (1928), the Randolph Wells Building (1928), and the US Customs House (1932), although the Carbide and Carbon Building, by far their most renowned building, is the only one the Chicago Art Deco Society has classified as an Art Deco skyscraper.

The most distinctive characteristic of the Carbide and Carbon Building, as the *Tribune* explained, was its use of color, which made it an "exception." The first four floors are faced with shiny polished black granite, the thirty-nine floors above that base are different shades of mottled green terra-cotta, and the pinnacle, or campanile, is adorned with gold leaf. It has often been said the glittering campanile was designed to resemble a foil-wrapped champagne bottle, but many commentators have argued this is a classic urban myth. Except it's not. Daniel Burnham Jr. recounted in his diary that, in a meeting with the representatives of the Carbide and Carbon Company, they told him they wanted something like the American Radiator Building in New York (1924), which has a terra-cotta crown embellished with gold leaf, but in "black trimmed with gold . . . the black to be the color

An Art Deco logo of interlocking C's, one in reverse, occurs throughout the Carbide and Carbon Building, as seen here on the bronze elevator doors. Photograph by the author.

in an old champagne bottle."[2] The company approved a model of the building at the end of June 1929. The gold leaf on the fifty-foot campanile is real 24-karat gold, although it is a mere 1/5000 of an inch thick. The campanile is ringed with hexagonal medallions and extensive golden Art Deco trim. In the words of skyscraper historian Joseph J. Korom Jr., "The top of the Carbide and Carbon is nothing less than a treat for the eyes—a reward for searching out beauty."[3] Illumination of the building's pinnacle only added to the visual excitement.

The tower above the black granite base is dark

green terra-cotta with gold terra-cotta trim accenting the pilasters and piers. Recessed vertical strips containing the windows run unbroken from base to campanile, emphasizing the building's verticality. The dark base was brightened by the addition of attractive bronze trimming, a stylistic feature that carries into the dramatic two-story lobby, which is a travertine-lined Art Deco showcase of bronze, Tennessee marble, and a type of black marble called "Noir Belge" ("Belgian Black"), one of the most expensive marbles in the world, an indication that the Carbide and Carbon Co. was not cutting corners. All the metal features—elevator doors, shop fronts, mailboxes, the trim on the pilasters—are polished bronze. The tall glass entryway is recessed and ringed with black marble, and the large window above the doors sports a delicate abstract Art Deco design featuring two C's, one in reverse (interlocking C's are also on the elevator doors). In addition, in Korom's words, "The walls of floors thirty-five through thirty-seven are celebratory, they express Art Deco geometrics, the zigzags, the concentric circles and cascading forms." The building was constructed with a garage in the basement with parking for forty cars, a forward-looking feature for the 1920s.

After World War II delayed necessary maintenance, a much-needed $350,000 restoration project was done in 1948. Union Carbide sold the building in 1957, and it has changed hands a couple of times since. The Whiston Group bought it for $4 million in 1965. The Carbide and Carbon Building was given Chicago landmark status in 1996, and in the twenty-first century it, like the Chicago Motor Club down the street, found new life as a hotel. When Hard Rock International took over the building in 2004, it underwent a restoration to the tune of $106 million (partly funded by city and county tax incentives and $16 million in historic preservation credits from the federal government). Blair Kamin, architecture critic for the *Chicago Tribune*, said at the time that the project was "a match made in architectural heaven, pairing a distinctive building with a distinctive hotel, and, in the process, restoring the multi-colored glory of a once-ragged landmark skyscraper."[4] Although the *Chicago Tribune* had called it a "Green 'nd Gold Tower" in 1928, by 2000 accumulated smoke and soot had made it more of a "Black 'nd Gold Tower." A thorough cleaning, however, restored its variegated dark green tint. The bronze trim and granite were restored, and a seven-story addition was put on the building's south side. The old lobby was, thankfully, left intact, but a respectful new lobby was added on the Wacker Place side. The replacement gold on the campanile was, like the original, 24 karats.

The building was sold again in 2018 and became the St. Jane Hotel, after Chicago's revered social work pioneer Jane Addams. Two years later, it briefly shut its doors because of the COVID-19 pandemic. In October 2020 it was purchased by the Montage International hotel development company, after which it reopened as the Pendry Chicago Hotel. Specialty suites were opened on the top floors, so that anyone who is so inclined may sleep in the neck of a champagne bottle.

When the Carbide and Carbon Building underwent renovations in the early twenty-first century, the original Art Deco lobby on Michigan Avenue seen here was retained, although a respectful new lobby was added on Wacker Place. Photograph by the author.

The Drake

No. 7

PALMOLIVE BUILDING

HOLABIRD & ROOT, 1929

To appreciate the difference between American architecture in the 1920s and the 1950s, it's enlightening to compare the Palmolive Building in Chicago, built in 1929, to the Colgate-Palmolive Building in New York City, built in 1955.[1] The first, the headquarters of the Colgate-Palmolive-Peet Company (as it was known), was designed by the firm of Holabird & Root in the American-bred skyscraper style known at the time as "moderne" and today as Art Deco; the second, at Park Avenue and 50th Street, is in the "International Style" brought to America's shores predominantly by German-born architect Ludwig Mies van der Rohe, whose motto was "less is more." The contrast between the two buildings says a lot about changing tastes. The Colgate-Palmolive corporate headquarters in New York was one of the buildings that came under the purview of Frank Lloyd Wright, America's most famous architect, who toured Park Avenue in a hansom cab in the 1950s and came away saying, "These buildings are . . . poetry-crushers . . . posters, probably, for some kind of business or other, but for God's sakes, don't call it architecture . . . call it modern, but don't call it new."[2]

The Colgate-Palmolive Building in New York City, built in the International Style of the 1950s, makes a contrast to the 1929 Palmolive Building in Chicago. Photograph by Beyond My Ken, https://commons.wikimedia.org/wiki/File:Colgate-Palmolive_Building_300_Park_Avenue.jpg. CC BY-SA 4.0 https://creativecommons.org/licenses/by-sa/4.0/deed.en.

Back when the *Chicago Tribune* reported the Palmolive Building was being planned, real estate editor Al Chase got a little carried away with the soap metaphors—"Upper Michigan Avenue is to have a 42 story monument to cleanliness—a soaring suds skyscraper, lathered into steel, stone and stability."[3] He reported the purchase price of the lot to be $1.5 million, or $50 per square foot.

The Palmolive Building was constructed during one of the worst winters on record in Chicago. Writing in *Architectural Forum* in 1930, Henry J. B. Hoskins said,

> The principal point of interest would appear to lie in the speed of its erection in the face of unusually severe weather conditions. . . . Located on the edge of Lake Michigan, the Palmolive Building presented a perfect target for the zero winds that came tearing down over the 360-mile open stretch of water to the north. Under these conditions working upon the scaffolds was impossible, and men working upon open floors were often lashed to beams to prevent them from being blown overboard. It was impossible to hoist steel or stone, and then on calm days men had to employ blow torches to melt away the snow and ice. In spite of this, the definite building schedules were adhered to and with very few accidents.[4]

When the building opened, much of the attention it received had to do with its location at the northern end of Michigan Avenue, which completed the extension of the boulevard from the Loop, Chicago's central business district, to the Gold Coast, its most exclusive residential neighborhood. The *Chicago Tribune*

The Palmolive Building really was erected in "all kinds of weather" during one of the worst Chicago winters.

Tenant in Palmolive Building detected with bar of Ivory Soap

Humorists of the day had fun with the idea that the Palmolive skyscraper was built by a soap company. Author's collection.

opined that the building "marks what will probably be for many years to come the dividing line between purely residential and commercial Chicago."[5] Only a few years before, this part of Chicago was considered too far from downtown to warrant skyscraper construction. According to Hoskins, in 1930, "With the advantages of rapid transportation to all parts of the city, the exhilaration of clear skies and the close proximity to delightful residential centers, it's not remarkable that the Colgate-Palmolive-Peet Company should erect a towering landmark as a distinctive termination to this north side gateway of Chicago."[6] Because the building was perceived as distant from the smoky air of downtown, it was dubbed a "monument to that schoolgirl complexion," playing off a Palmolive Soap advertising slogan of the Jazz Age: "Keep That Schoolgirl Complexion." A reviewer in *The New York Times* couldn't resist the hygiene metaphor: "The Palmolive Building is as trim and clean in its lines as are the cakes of soap that brought it into being."[7]

The thirty-seven-story Palmolive Building (not forty-two, as the *Tribune* announced) is a characteristic setback skyscraper, although it's novel in that it features both vertical and horizontal setbacks. The deeply set vertical bays create vivid channels on the facade while setback floors offer terraces.[8] According to architectural historian John W. Stamper, "these recessed bays are relatively shallow in the lower masses but are deeply indented in the tower rising above the seventeenth floor. The visual result of both the setbacks and the recessed bays is a rhythmic play of projecting and receding limestone surfaces that avoids the kind of boxy look in which one building seems to stand on top of another."[9] Dark terra-cotta decorative spandrels with stylized papyrus motifs between the bays constitute one of the few purely decorative features. The first and second stories on the north and west sides contain two-story metal-framed storefronts originally framed in cast iron; the rest of the tower is Indiana limestone.[10]

For a brief time the Palmolive Building was the second-tallest building in the Windy City—the Chicago Temple Building was the tallest, by only four feet, until the Chicago Board of Trade Building surpassed it in 1930. The caissons supporting the tower stand on bedrock. The original windows were double-hung (a significant plus in the days before air-conditioning), framed in steel, and glazed with plate glass. The *Tribune* praised the long, narrow, and abundant windows because they meant "every worker enjoys day long daylight—and no eye strain."[11] The ceilings were higher than average at ten feet seven inches, which, the builders said, would enhance the cooling effect of the lake breezes. The tapering of the building means that the square footage of the floors diminishes markedly with height:

» Floor one: 15,885 sq. ft.
» Floors two to ten: 11,850 sq. ft.
» Floors eleven to sixteen: 10,500 sq. ft.
» Floors seventeen to twenty-one: 5,800 sq. ft.
» Floors twenty-two to thirty-two: 4,100 sq. ft.
» Floors thirty-three and thirty-four: 3,842 sq. ft.
» Floors thirty-five and thirty-six: 3,196 sq. ft.
» Floor thirty-seven: 2,914 sq. ft.

The developers saw this rising diminishment as a selling point. According to the original rental brochure, tenants who leased a whole floor at one of the setback levels "may use them as promenades and if they so desire, beautify them with formal planting." Also, renters who wished to occupy an entire floor had a wide choice of sizes. As an advertisement expressed it, "firms of widely varying space requirements have been able to select a floor which they can occupy entirely, with consequent efficiency, saving and impressiveness."[12] The Colgate-Palmolive-Peet Company itself occupied the first eight floors and effortlessly rented the rest of the building to prestige tenants. Its desirability can be assessed from its being almost fully occupied throughout the Great Depression.

The Wrigley Building, still well known for its exterior radiance, initiated something of a fashion for floodlit buildings in Chicago. An article in *Architectural Forum* in 1930 observed, "The use of floodlights as an advertising medium for commercial structures is a comparatively new but important and constantly increasing practice."[13] As Mark J. Bouman expressed it, "From the start, tower construction went hand in hand with illumination; from the start, the romantic landscape thus created became richly symbolic, evocative of America's progressiveness, modernity, and technical precocity."[14] A local firm, Curtis Lighting Company, was known as the nation's "pioneer of indirect illumination."

The elevator doors of the Palmolive Building were done by Mexican-born artist Enrique Alférez. Photograph by the author.

The Palmolive Building was perfect for such treatment, and 372 light-beaming projectors were installed, the setbacks being used as lighting platforms.[15] The luminous effect generated the nickname "La Tour d'Ar-

gent" ("The Silver Tower"). Accordingly, the owners opened three "Tour d'Argent" eating places: the Tour d'Argent Fountain Lunch Room, the Tour d'Argent Dining Room, and the Tour d'Argent Coffee Shop. Tour d'Argent was (and still is) the name of a café in Paris. According to the *Chicago Tribune*, John Holabird and John Root trekked all the way there, where "they do know how to fix up a dinner," to "gather ideas."[16] Such were the sacrifices hard-working Art Deco architects had to make.

In 1965, *Playboy* magazine leased ten floors of the Palmolive Building and advertised its presence with nine-foot-tall illuminated letters at the top of the tower. Photograph by Victor Albert Grigas, https://flickr.com/photos/140897960@N03/25318157247. CC BY-SA 2.0, https://creativecommons.org/licenses/by-sa/2.0/deed.en.

The first floor was first-class. Shops and restaurants lined the interior. The lobby floors were of Tennessee marble, and the walls featured a base of red Notre Dame marble quarried in France, with Circassian walnut above. The elevator doors showcased carved

The Palmolive Building's two-billion-candlepower beacon, the brightest in the world, was featured on many Chicago postcards. Author's collection.

bas-reliefs of Native American women by the Mexican-born artist Enrique Alférez (1901–1999), a student of sculptor Lorado Taft at the Art Institute of Chicago.

When the building underwent an unfortunate remodeling of the first fifteen floors in the 1960s, these doors were all that remained of the original ground-floor interior. The despoilment was the work of the Playboy Corporation, which leased the building from 1965 to 1990 and occupied ten floors. The company installed "PLAYBOY" in nine-foot-tall illuminated letters across the top of the edifice.

In 1982 the base was altered, as the original Addison gabbro (a coarse-grained igneous rock) cladding was removed.[17] The retail stores have also undergone considerable changes over the years. Despite the alterations, the report on the building by the National Register of Historic Places states,

> The Palmolive Building retains excellent integrity. All four facades of the building appear as original, with all original exterior masonry and Terra Cotta features of the 3rd through the 37th stories remaining in good condition. In addition, the original steel and aluminum beacon mast has been preserved. Key features of the storefronts such as the openings and the double-height design, the attached columns with illuminated terminations, and upper level spandrels have all been preserved. In the interior, the artistry of sculptor Enrique Alférez and the ornamental nickel stairs have remained at the first floor, in addition to the elegant executive offices of the 37th floor.

For a half century, the defining characteristic of the building was not its illuminated facade or its schoolgirl complexion, but the two-billion-candlepower beacon, the brightest in the world, installed in August 1930. The light, which had a lens eighty inches in diameter, cost $50,000 and was manufactured in Brooklyn, New York. It sat atop a sixty-five-foot-tall aluminum-clad steel tower and was switched on by President Herbert Hoover, who pushed a button in the White House. It was said it could be seen from a high-flying plane five hundred miles away. Claims that it could be seen in Milwaukee were journalistic hyperbole, however. In fact, when the beacon was first lit, observers atop a six-story building in Michigan City, Indiana, said they were unable to spot it. The magazine *Modern Mechanics and Inventions* published a helpful drawing explaining that, pitched two degrees above the horizon as it was, the beam would strike the horizon thirty-three miles from Chicago (Milwaukee is ninety miles away). The light was initially meant to be called the Lindbergh Beacon, but when the celebrated aviator declined the honor, it was renamed the Palmolive Beacon (it was reported that the publicity-shy Lindy skipped the lighting ceremony due to "a desire to avoid reporters and news cameramen"). Sadly, Elmer G. Sperry, president of the Sperry Gyroscope Company, who had developed the technology that made the beacon possible and then donated the funds for it, never saw it lit—he died two months before.

The beacon was a familiar Chicago sight featured on postcards until the surrounding area was developed and even taller towers became its neighbors. Residents of these new structures began to complain that the intense brightness was blinding them, and the beacon was replaced in 2007 by a smaller light that swiveled over a small part of the lake and even then only on Saturday and Sunday between sundown and 11 p.m. The Palmolive Beacon is often said to have been the first to top a Chicago skyscraper, but searchlights atop a steel tower forty-five feet above the roof of the Roanoke Building on La Salle Street were first switched on in July 1928.

In January 1930, the Lake Shore Trust and Savings Bank awarded the Palmolive Building a gold medal for being the most beautiful building in the North Central district that year. Holabird & Root thus captured the honor for the second consecutive year, having been awarded the prize in 1929 for 333 North Michigan.

Nº. 8

CHICAGO DAILY NEWS BUILDING

HOLABIRD & ROOT, 1929

In the late 1920s, the *Chicago Daily News*, the most popular newspaper in the Windy City, was squeezed into what looked like a modest apartment building with a cheap restaurant on the ground floor. The publication, with a daily circulation north of four hundred thousand and a staff of two thousand, badly needed a new home. Publisher Walter A. Strong hired the best: Holabird & Root, who had so recently brought the Art Deco style to Chicago architecture with 333 North Michigan and the Chicago Motor Club building. They would repeat their success for the *Daily News*.

The precise term "mass media," or just "media," dates from the Art Deco era, when radio became prevalent, but mass media itself began a century before with the rise of the penny press. While papers previously cost about six cents, the advent of steam-powered printing presses and the switch from rag-based paper to wood-based paper meant newspapers could be sold for just one cent. Penny papers achieved huge circulations as the number of newspapers in the United States climbed from two hundred in 1800 to three thousand in 1860. The august *New York Times* began as a penny paper. So did the *Chicago Daily News*.

The wild and wacky days of Chicago newspaperdom were immortalized in the fast-paced Broadway comedy *The Front Page* by reporters Ben Hecht and Charles MacArthur. Hecht's main job was penning a column in the *Daily News* called "One Thousand and One Afternoons in Chicago." One of Hecht's discoveries was a young writer named Carl Sandburg, who worked for the paper for most of the 1920s, mostly doing movie reviews. Meanwhile, he was writing poems, one of which dubbed Chicago the "City of the Big Shoulders."

In 1926 a *Daily News* writer named Fred A. Chappell wrote a description of the swiftly changing state of the newspaper business in the first decades of the twentieth century:

> There are new wars, new leaders, new customs, new issues, new catch words, new problems, new drinks, new nuisances, new managers, a kaleidoscopic procession of new editors, new reporters and new and improved methods of presenting the news. The old chalk plate and the line drawing give place to the halftone. Improved presses are built, the paper expands in size. Telegraph news assume increasing importance. The readers become more cosmopolitan.
>
> Departments of the newspaper become more sharply differentiated. Increased specialization is the watchword. The man who can do everything fairly well is supplanted by the man who can do one or two things better. . . . The modern age has arrived.[1]

When the new Daily News Building opened on July 8, 1929, observers found two aspects especially praiseworthy: the building was the first in Chicago to make use of air rights and a public plaza.

What are air rights? This legal theory, which dates to the Middle Ages, holds that the owner of a property also owns the rights to the space above it—reaching as high as heaven itself. Therefore, the owner can sell or lease the airspace above their property without selling the parcel itself and still use the property for its original purpose. A major precedent was set in 1913 when the newly built Grand Central Terminal in New York City made use of the air rights of the railroads whose tracks were beneath the terminal. In fact, when the concept of air rights began to be used in American cities, it applied not to *any* parcel of land but only to the space above "railroad tracks and facilities."[2] Air rights were, in many ways, a win-win-win situation: the railroads made money from leasing the space, the developers were spared the pains of demolishing existing above-ground properties, and the city benefited from the covering up of train yards and the subsequent noise reduction.[3]

The Daily News Building was also built above railroad tracks. While the trains continued to run on the tracks, caissons were sunk between them, from platforms above. The rear part of the building was erected upon these caissons. The excavated earth was transported on viaducts to the nearby Chicago River, where it was loaded onto barges.

There was, however, one problem that didn't exist in Manhattan. The trains beneath Grand Central Terminal were electrified. The trains that went in and out of Chicago were pulled by smoke-belching steam locomotives. An ingenious engineer named Joshua D'Esposito devised the solution. Over each individual track he designed arched rows separated by open slots that collected the rising smoke into a five-foot-tall smoke chamber over the entire track area. As described at the time, "The chamber . . . might be referred to as the base of the large double shaft or smokestack that runs through the full height of the building, where the smoke, decreased in density and quantity, is discharged into the air."[4] Because the gas emitted by the locomotives would quickly eat away at steel, the smoke chamber had to be lined with a special type of dense concrete. The work was done during icy weather. To keep the concrete from freezing, workers used portable heating units called salamanders and covered the newly poured concrete with marsh hay.[5]

The public plaza, still enjoyed by users today, was trailblazing because Chicagoans of the time hardly thought of their foul-smelling river, choked with barges and tugboats, as a recreational area. Previously, most commercial enterprises turned their backs to the river. Yet the plaza was conceived of as a public space. As publisher Strong put it in a newspaper ad, "Our new home, necessitated by your growing preference, is your home. We want you to visit it . . . enjoy it with us." In the plaza's early days, nightly band concerts were held there, and in 1934 the Mormon Tabernacle Choir performed (traffic was tied up for blocks around). Yet it wasn't until the administration of Mayor Richard M. Daley that people finally began envisioning the river as "Chicago's Second Lakefront."

In typical Art Deco fashion, the twenty-six-story Daily News Building has a granite base and an Indiana limestone upper section. The window and door surrounds are bronze. Vertical lines are repeated on the facade and on the buttressed ends, and according to reviewer Anne Lee in *Architectural Forum*, the vertical effect is "again introduced in the topmost set-back section, above a strong horizontal line, with an interesting combination of vertical and horizontal effects at the top of the structure."[6]

The three distinct horizontal sections of the building reflect their original functions. The seven-story base contained the printing plant, along with editorial and business offices. The floors above consisted of rentable office space—when the building opened, the offices of the Chicago and North Western Railway occupied the first eight floors of this section. The top three floors contained lounges, each with a terrace, along with the broadcasting facilities of WMAQ, the newspaper's radio station, and (this was really looking ahead) a television broadcasting studio. The building has two lobbies—one on the ground floor and one on the second—and together they make one of Chicago's grandest Art Deco spaces. The walls are made of Bottocino marble, an oystershell-colored stone with white veins and spots that is quarried in the Brescia region of Italy, while the floors are black and gray terrazzo. The elaborately decorated elevator doors are of nickel silver, which is a copper alloy that, despite its name, contains no silver but has a silvery sheen. The grillwork on the staircase banisters is particularly fine, especially considering most visitors use the elevators rather than the stairs.

At the center of the plaza is the imposing Victor F. Lawson Memorial Fountain, named after the manager and owner of the *Daily News* from 1876 until his death in 1925 (he was also one of the founders of the Associated Press). Author Greg Borzo calls it one of the city's "forgotten fountains"—one of those fountains "still in place but not known or recognized as fountains and unlikely to ever operate again."[7] Too bad: it was quite a sight with water surging from its three twenty-five-foot-high portals into its large ground-level basin.

One of the most attractive features of the building's exterior is its extensive sculptural program. The ornamentation consists mostly of limestone bas-reliefs that are the work of Alvin W. Meyer, the head of the Holabird & Root sculpture department, who later supplied even more impressive sculptures for another Holabird & Root building, the Chicago Board of Trade Building. Among the reliefs are stylized portraits of famous figures in the history of journalism: Benjamin Franklin, Charles Anderson Dana, Horace Greeley, Joseph Pulitzer, Samuel Bowles, James Gordon Bennett, Joseph Medill (of the rival *Chicago Tribune*, no less), and of course, Victor Lawson. Other sculptural designs depict the history of writing: a man of the Stone Age carving with a hammer and chisel, "An Ancient Scribe," and depictions of the first printing press and the linotype machine. Meyer also fashioned patterns based on old printers' marks—snake, bull, rooster, boat—which were, in a sense, logos used by printers to identify their work.

Art historian Teri J. Edelstein has suggested that the ornamentation in the lobby of One North La Salle (see chapter 14) might have been partly influenced by the distinctive work of the French ironworker (*ferronier*) Edgar Brandt, the master of Art Deco iron design.[8] This is not unlikely, yet the decorations in the Daily News Building are more strikingly similar to Brandt's designs and appear to be inspired by his most famous creation, the large five-panel iron and brass screen called "The Oasis" (c. 1926). Brandt exercised a strong influence on American artists, especially with his work on the Madison Belmont Building in Manhattan (1924–1925), where he created the

This spread: A decorative grille in the Daily News Building appears to show the influence of "The Oasis" (c. 1926), the acclaimed iron and brass screen by the master French ironworker Edgar Brandt. Grille photograph by the author; Brandt screen from Wikimedia Commons.

framing around the entrance doors and the exterior bulkhead grilles, work that has been called "one of the first instances of Art Deco architectural design in the United States."[9] In 1925, Marshall Field's department store mounted a State Street window display of silks inspired by Brandt's art, along with "representative pieces of M. Brandt's delicately wrought iron grille work." (Could "The Oasis" have been one of them?) And in a review of a show at the Art Institute in May 1926, Eleanor Jewett of the *Chicago Tribune* singled out "the delicate and graceful screens by Edgar Brandt" as "objects of special worth."[10] It's difficult to imagine that Chicago's design community would have failed to attend, and learn from, this exhibition.

But the glory of the Daily News Building was its mural, which more than one critic has called "the Sistine Chapel of Chicago." It was the chef d'oeuvre of John Warner Norton (see chapters 1 and 2). Mary Lackritz Gray has written that the 180-by-18-foot masterpiece Norton fashioned in 1929 for the *Daily News*, which depicted across three sections the process of creating a newspaper, is, or was, "possibly the nation's longest mural."[11] It comprised nineteen panels that covered 3,300 square feet. Norton painted them

one at a time in his studio (he never worked on-site), and they were then glued to the ceiling. The mural decorated the concourse that linked the Daily News Building to a train station, and hundreds of commuters viewed it every day. In 2004, architecture critic Blair Kamin said:

> The design broke decisively with static classical murals, which relied on allegorical figures and beaux-arts imagery. Instead, it served up the same sort of machine-age dynamism that inspired streamlined trains and the zigzag motifs of Art Deco office buildings: A panoply of typewriters, telegraph machines and airplanes arranged on a field of criss-crossing diagonals.
>
> These diagonals, which suggested airplane beacons knifing through the sky, lined up perfectly with the pilasters, or flattened columns, along the walls of the concourse. Like banner headlines, big blocks of type spelled out the three sections of the mural: "Gathering the News," "Printing the News" and "Transporting the News."
>
> The result was an extraordinary integration of art and architecture, a grand gateway into Chicago.

Gray explains that water leaking from above began to damage the artwork, and the mural was removed in 1993 with plans to have it restored. Yet the mural was apparently left to languish in an unknown Chicago-area warehouse. A subsequent owner of the building, Sam Zell, said he planned to reinstall the Norton mural, but as time dragged on, Robert Sideman of Landmarks Illinois grumbled that Zell's strategy for dealing with the public on the matter of the mural was to "say all the right things and do nothing." The mural has since been found at Mana Contemporary, an art exhibition and performance space in Chicago.[12]

Beginning in the 1950s, the fortunes of the *Chicago Daily News* declined. It was an afternoon paper, and its demise was primarily attributed to increased competition for Chicagoans' evenings. People were going out more—to restaurants, sports events, theaters—but the main culprit was television. It also didn't help that

TRANSPORTING THE NEWS
CHICAGO DAILY NEWS
DAILY NEWS
THE CHICAGO
THE CHICAGO DAILY NEWS
PRINTING THE NEWS

This spread: "The Sistine Chapel of Chicago" was a label given the expansive ceiling mural in the Daily News Building created by Chicago artist John Warner Norton. The mural was removed in 1993. Chicago Daily News Building (1928), Chicago, Illinois. Holabird and Root, architects. Historic Architecture and Landscape Image Collection, Ryerson and Burnham Art and Architecture Archives, The Art Institute of Chicago. Digital File # 24358 and # M525350.

The Victor F. Lawson Memorial Fountain, no longer working, was, with its twenty-five-foot-high waterfall, one of the most impressive fountains in Chicago. Chicago Daily News Building (1928), Chicago, Illinois. Holabird and Root, architects. Historic Architecture and Landscape Image Collection, Ryerson and Burnham Art and Architecture Archives, The Art Institute of Chicago. Digital File # 24357.

A series of relief panels on the Daily News Building depicts stages in the history of writing. Photograph by the author.

many commuters who used to read the paper heading home on trains and buses were now driving out to the suburbs on new expressways, getting their news from car radios. In 1959, Field Enterprises, headed by Marshall Field IV, bought the newspaper and moved it to the definitely non-Deco Chicago Sun-Times Building, which Field owned. Attempts to attract readers by means of new features didn't pan out, and the last edition of the grand old paper, winner of fifteen Pulitzer Prizes, was issued on March 4, 1978, with a headline reading "So Long, Chicago."

The newspaper had died. Would the building follow? It is now known as Two North Riverside Plaza, although architectural histories and guides generally still refer to it as the Chicago Daily News Building. As difficult as it is to imagine today, there was a time when plans were being hatched to remodel the Daily News Building into unrecognizability or raze it altogether. In 1975 the real estate tycoon Sam Zell acquired the structure. Zell had made his fortune buying distressed properties from developers in financial straits (he called himself "The Grave Dancer"). His plan to tear the building down did not find favor with Mayor Richard M. Daley, so Zell floated the idea of plopping a skyscraper down onto the plaza, which would have destroyed the access to the riverfront that made the plaza so valued in the first place. He also considered turning the building into condominiums and hanging balconies on the facade. None of this happened. The Great Recession of 2008 squelched any plans, and Zell declared bankruptcy at the end of the year.

UBS
CIVIC OPERA BUILDING
ONLY

Nº. 9

CIVIC OPERA HOUSE

GRAHAM, ANDERSON, PROBST & WHITE, 1929

The world's great opera houses (London, New York, Paris, Munich, Milan, Rome, Sydney, Vienna, and so on) tend to be freestanding buildings. Chicago's opera house is on the bottom floor of a skyscraper. But if it weren't so situated, opera in the Windy City might have failed to launch. The first resident opera companies in Chicago kept going broke.

Opera was first heard in Chicago as early as 1850, but the theater caught fire the day after the inaugural performance and burned down.[1] Another Chicago opera house went up in flames during the Great Chicago Fire of 1871. Eventually, Chicago opera found safer surroundings—the magnificent (and fireproof) Auditorium Building of 1889.

The Chicago Grand Opera Company, the city's first permanent resident company, was founded in 1910, only to go bankrupt in four years. It was succeeded in 1915 by the Chicago Opera Association, which in 1921 named as its director Mary Garden, a great Scottish-born lyric soprano who had moved to Chicago with her parents when she was eleven. Garden enjoyed playing the maverick. When she returned from a trip to Europe in the fall of 1921 with her hair bobbed, she told reporters, "Skirts should be as high as possible and hair as short as possible."[2] One of the most surprising episodes of her tenure was the commissioning of an opera from the modernist Russian composer Sergei Prokofiev. His adaptation of an eighteenth-century Italian comedy titled *The Love for Three Oranges* premiered at the Auditorium Theatre on December 31, 1921. It got a standing ovation, and at the post-performance party the composer "immediately downed three cocktails and got pleasantly tipsy."[3] Yet producing Prokofiev's opera was hugely expensive and it was reported that the company had lost one million dollars in one season. Another bust.

The opera was reorganized in 1922 as the Chicago Civic Opera and its backers enlisted as president a man who knew a great deal about finance—Samuel Insull, the tycoon who began his career as Thomas Edison's secretary and went on to found Commonwealth Edison and build an electrical utility empire. He kept a sharp eye on the new company's spending, but patrons complained that the productions were chintzy and the company was unable to attract the best singers. And, although Insull insisted opera was for everyone, he believed it had to make money. The solution: build an opera house that paid for itself.

In January 1927, Insull announced the new Civic Opera House would be built on the Chicago River between Washington and Madison Streets at 20 North Wacker Drive—an area that housed wholesale food dealers, which meant the land was relatively affordable. The wholesale market district was moved across the river. As a skyscraper with a theater at the bottom, it was, as the *Chicago Tribune* put it, "a building that should eventually pay for itself and pay for the opera."[4] The newspaper also said management would therefore be freed from "the need to respond to the changing demands of popular taste or to the protests of critical judgment," which leads to "undue conservatism and inhospitality to new ideas."[5]

The architectural firm that designed the new opera house, Graham, Anderson, Probst & White (GAPW), was prestigious; a main reason was its boss, Ernest Graham (1868–1938), who was considered the architectural heir of Daniel Burnham after Burnham's death in 1912. Graham eventually took control of Burnham's firm and, with new partners, renamed it Graham, Anderson, Probst & White. In the first decades of the twentieth century GAPW was known for its conservative classical Beaux-Arts style, but in the 1920s it moved steadily toward the Art Deco aesthetic and had embraced it fully by the time it designed the Civic Opera House and the Merchandise Mart.[6]

As planned, the building was to have two theaters—the large opera house and an 878-seat Civic Theater that would generate income by being leased out. (Over time, the Civic Theater proved too small and was incorporated into the large house as rehearsal space in 1996.) The profitable office building above would bring in rental income. This was a relatively new idea but hardly original to Insull. According to architectural historian Sally A. Kitt Chappell, the scheme of enclosing various facilities within a skyscraper was a growing—and very American—idea: "It was a period when banks, churches, colleges, department stores, libraries, meeting halls, and monuments were frequently tucked into or on top of a steel-framed office building."[7] The Auditorium Theatre is itself part of a much larger building. Another reason Insull favored the arrangement was that opera in Chicago would not rely on government subsidies, as in Europe. His conviction that opera was for everyone made him insist the building be accessible by public transportation; it was near two surface lines, an L station, and two railroad depots while having frontage ample enough for forty taxicabs. The plan for a plaza was not realized; instead, the building is fronted by an imposing seventeen-bay colonnade supported by thirty-five-foot-tall octagonal columns. The elaborate classical lunettes above the doorways are not especially Art Deco but are like those at the Paris Opera.

The relative narrowness of the site made a tall tower imperative. The original plan as conceived by Alfred Shaw, GAPW's chief designer, was to have the building surround a light court, with the theater below—a kind of square donut in which the side of the building fronting the river would also contain office space. As recounted by designer Clifford Noonan, however, "One day Mr. Graham came in just loaded for bear and said 'We're going to start all over. Eliminate the office space on the river side of the building entirely and go up with a higher tower on the Wacker Drive side.'"[8] The staff redid the whole thing, and the result was a Ushaped edifice featuring a forty-five-story tower with a pyramidal roof flanked by two twenty-two-story wings that wrap around the thirteen-story auditorium—a conception that transmuted a potentially good building into one of Chicago's Art Deco finest.

The final design, as many people noted, looked like a colossal armchair, which led to a myth that won't go away: that of "Insull's throne." Many commentators (and tour guides) have repeated that the Civic Opera House was given that moniker because only a throne was fitting for the domineering mogul. Although many sources aver that the building was "quickly" or "instantly" called "Insull's throne," the first uses appear to date from the early 1960s. The myth might have originated with one John Glickman, who was a stagehand at the opera house for some forty years. In 1960, during a lawsuit over the ownership of the Auditorium Building, he was asked why the opera company, which performed in the perfectly fine Auditorium Theatre for years, had felt the need to build a new opera house. (The offstage areas of the Auditorium stage were in fact much too small for modern opera stagings.) He blamed Insull: "Did you ever see the opera house from a plane or helicopter? From up there, the building looks like a huge throne. . . . Insull built the Opera Building because he wanted a throne . . . a monument."[9] That recounting of an event that supposedly happened three decades previously, with no explanation of Glickman's access to Insull's intentions, is not especially persuasive.

The original "Insull's throne" was in fact the Commonwealth Edison Building on Clark and Adams Streets (a.k.a. the Edison Building; originally the Commercial National Bank Building). A newspaper article from May 9, 1934, that explained how two clever financiers seized control of the edifice from Insull was titled "Undermined Insull's Throne."[10] Besides, the Civic Opera House isn't the only Jazz Age Chicago building that looks like a chair: so do the Field Building, the Board of Trade Building, and the Chicago Daily News Building. The arrangement was a rational way of maximizing the amount of light coming through the windows; for high-quality buildings it was recommended that the maximum distance between a window and an interior wall be twenty-four feet.[11]

The avenue in front of the building was disfigured by a nonoperational line of elevated railroad tracks that was used to store passenger cars during the day until they were needed during rush hour. This eyesore was an affront to John "Bathhouse" Coughlin, one of those colorful Chicago aldermen (like his partner "Hinky Dink" Kenna) who happily boosted his bank account while doing generous favors for constituents and championing civic improvements. He introduced a bill in the city council to have the tracks demolished, and so they were. As *The Chicagoan* explained, "Bath House John has occasionally showed symptoms of the soul of a poet."[12]

Unlike the Chicago Daily News Building across the river, the opera house turned its back on the polluted waterway. It's possible to visit it and not even realize it's on a riverbank. Nevertheless, it's an impressive edifice when seen from the other side of the river or from one of the nearby bridges. When paired with the Daily News Building, the result is a magisterial riparian spectacle. In 1933 an observer remarked, "Chicagoans hope that some day the entire river front through the business district will be lined on both sides with beautiful buildings like these."[13]

Opening night was November 4, 1929, with a production of *Aida*, and Insull himself greeted patrons in the grand foyer. James O'Donnell Bennett of the *Tribune* wrote, "In its beauty, in its convenience, in its stateliness, which is not incompatible with intimacy, and in its vast mechanical equipment for the smooth and subtle presentation of the most difficult of musical forms, this opera house disarmed criticism."[14] Chicago's elite, who liked displaying their finery in the theater-circling boxes at the Auditorium Theatre, were dismayed to discover that the number of private boxes had declined from fifty-eight to thirty-six. As *The Chicagoan* observed, "twenty-two of the box holders in the old Auditorium will be compelled to descend from their former positions of social vantage and take their opera from orchestral chairs."[15] Nevertheless, the upper crust showed up in their regalia, and a battery of press photographers was there to record their entrance. The grand foyer provided sweeping staircases on which ladies could brandish their jewels and gowns. Robert Pollak, writing in *The Chicagoan*, spoke of "a glittering array of feminine haberdashery purchased with the paper profits of the late lamented bull market."

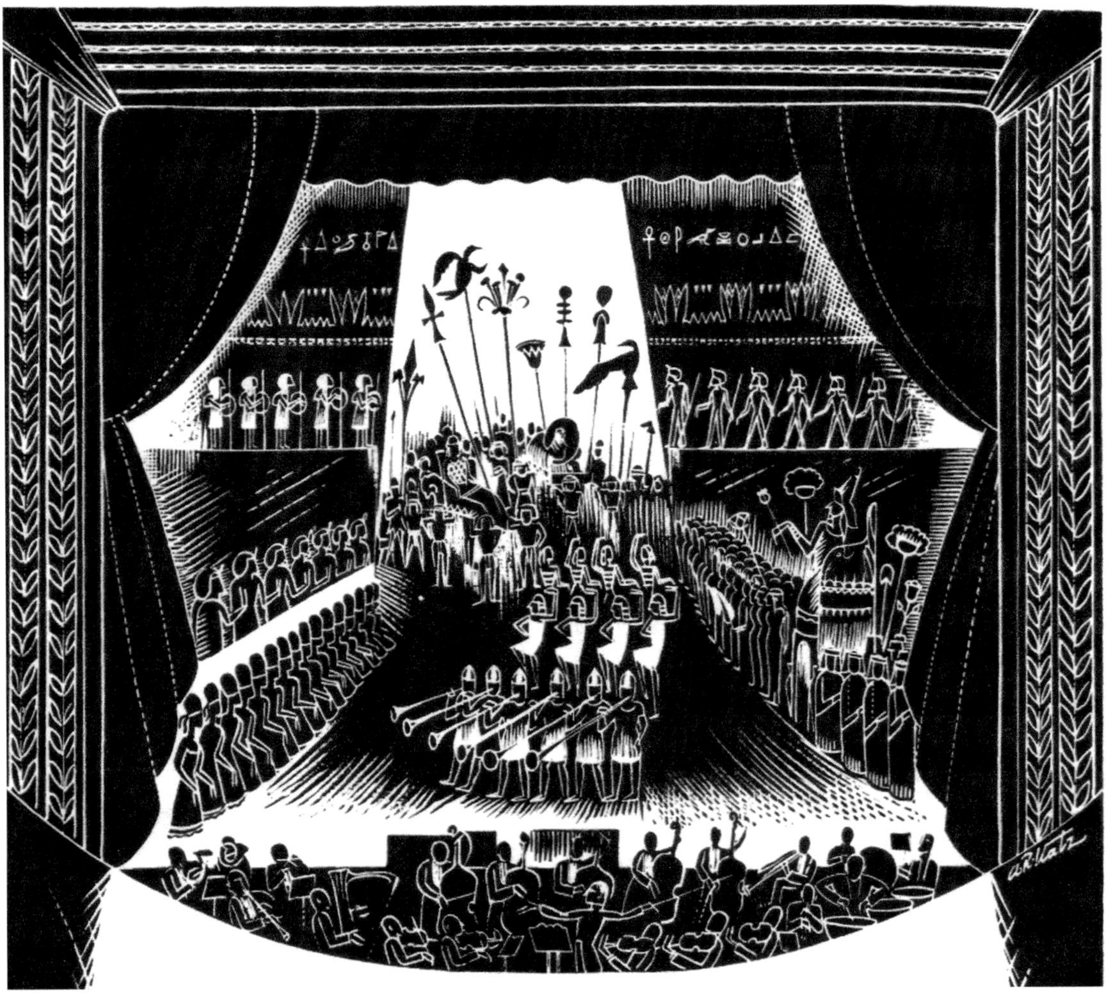

Above: Giuseppe Verdi's grand spectacle *Aida* was performed at the opening night of the opera, as interpreted in a playful cartoon from *The Chicagoan* magazine.

Opposite: The focal point of the capacious Art Deco auditorium of the Civic Opera House, with a seating capacity of nearly 3,500, is the colorful curtain designed by Jules Guérin. Author's collection.

But most important, the acoustics were judged to be a success. Pollak wrote: "The sounding board of wood and plaster at the base of the stage sends the tone of the orchestra back into the theatre with sonority and brilliance. The horns, in tutti passages, speak with rich mellowness. Strings, brass, and woodwinds, break into stillness on the downbeat as if cut out of existence by a knife. The theatre meets, with equal success, the subtle demands of the human voice. The most dulcet tones of soprano or tenor carry clearly and without echo to the last and most lofty seat in the house."

The enormous main floor was impressively deep, and although the seating capacity of the theater (3,472) was slightly less than the Auditorium Theatre's, nearly half the seats were on the main floor, whereas at the Auditorium only about a quarter were. Reviewers tended to comment more on the high-tech features that made possible innovative, realistic stagecraft than on the building itself. For example, the magazine *Through the Ages* said the stage was "one of the marvels of modern science. Nowhere is the mechanical and lighting equipment equaled. A fourteen-story building

P-20

A satyr pursuing a nymph is one of many Art Deco ornamental features in the opera house interior. Photograph by the author.

could be placed between the stage floor and the gridiron floor."[16] The gridiron, or grid, is a steel structure above the stage from which scenery and equipment are hung. The gridiron floor, at 145 feet above the stage, is indeed as high as Chicago's fourteen-story Reliance Building and is one of the highest in the world. The stage was a copious 120 feet wide, and the orchestra pit, which could be raised and lowered, could contain 120 musicians. John Augur Holabird Jr., scion of the rival firm Holabird & Root, grumbled that it was *too* big: "It makes a good movie house. It's kind of like Radio City Music Hall."[17] But, of course, his dad hadn't gotten the job.

The opera house contained an enormous costume department complete with a laundry. A special room contained hundreds of models for stage sets. Herbert M. Johnson, manager of the Civic Opera, boasted that the scenery department had "three huge floors, seventy feet by fifty feet, on which the canvas is laid flat and painted; then there are three upright frames, seventy feet by forty-five feet, which move up and down by electricity, so painters can stand on the floor and paint without having to climb on scaffolds. Even the garage, for housing the great trucks with which the scenery is carried to and from the opera house, is located in this studio warehouse."[18] *Popular Mechanics* magazine published a lavishly colored article on the technical wonders of the new house, while *Architectural Forum* devoted a special section of the April 1930 issue to them. Here one can learn that the reverberation time of the hall, when filled with operagoers, is 1.47 seconds; that the concrete caissons supporting the structure extend 115 feet below street level (the height of an eleven-story building); and that back of the stage was a "steam device" that could fill the entire scene with a "cloud effect."

As for the interior decor, which gets the most aesthetic interest today, Sally A. Kitt Chappell has commented, "the building is decorated with distinctive original ornament, restrained on the exterior but lavish on the interior in the Chicago manner."[19] According to opera historian Robert C. Marsh, the building's interior "was a gilded marble palace with a grand foyer

Art Deco light fixture in the Civic Opera House. Photograph by Andrea Blatz.

Left and following spread: Civic Opera House colonnades. Photographs by Ian McClellan.

encircled by a balcony at the level of the box seats, the two floors united by grand staircases worthy of any major European theater."[20] The grand foyer is forty-four feet high with a rose and gold ceiling and fluted piers lit by bronze torchieres, along with bronze and frosted glass Art Deco chandeliers, or pendant lights, made by the Sterling Bronze Company of New York.[21] The walls and floors are marble. "The auditorium," Chappell writes, "is lavishly decorated in a glowing color scheme. Gold covers most of the elaborately carved surfaces with touches of a palette of subtle mixtures of cadmium red and cadmium yellow light blended with vert emeraude [emerald green]."[22]

The overall effect of the auditorium is soothing and inspirational. One main attraction is the thirty-five-by-fifty-foot fire curtain designed by Jules Guérin, a "lively mural in shades of vermillion, salmon, and gold with accents of blue, green, and ivory" that "de-

picts characters from over forty operas as a crowd of merrymakers, dancers, and musicians waving banners and pennants, carrying lanterns, beating drums, clanging cymbals, and blowing horns."[23] Guérin was also responsible for the octagonal medallions atop the descending panels, the geometric designs on the grand foyer ceiling, and other interior touches. His work, as Mary Lackritz Gray has pointed out, is not out-and-out Art Deco, hearkening as it does to the Beaux-Arts era, but is definitely "compatible" with it.

Sadly, the plan for the building to pay the costs of opera went up in flames like Wagner's Valhalla. The house opened just six days after Black Tuesday (October 29, 1929), when a wave of panic selling touched off a stock market crash and launched the Great Depression. Both rental income and ticket sales nosedived. After the 1931–1932 season the opera went dark. Insull was indicted for securities fraud, and although he was acquitted of all charges, he died in 1938 of a heart attack in the Paris Metro. That he had but a few coins in his pocket has regularly been considered evidence that he was broke, but the Paris police suspected that his wallet had been stolen. Still, he was riding the subway and not in a taxi. Nevertheless, he died with the knowledge that, as a friend once told him, he'd "built a monument that they can't tear down."[24]

Unlike Insull, Chicago's opera community was not crushed by hard times. From 1933 to 1935 the company was reorganized as the Chicago Grand Opera Company. The stagings were done on a shoestring budget, and many complained that they looked like it. Then it became the Chicago City Opera Company (1936–1939) and, from 1940 to 1946, the Chicago Opera Company. Under all regimes, it was a financial struggle for opera in the Windy City. Between 1947 and 1953, Chicago had no resident opera company at all, but the Lyric Opera was created in 1954 and continues to this day. The Lyric Opera bought the building in 1993 and launched a $100 million restoration, in which the technical features were updated, the historic architecture was refurbished and preserved, and audience facilities, such as a new dining space, were upgraded. A new company meant a new name, and so they renamed the building the Lyric Opera House.

Nº. 10

FOREMAN STATE NATIONAL BANK

GRAHAM, ANDERSON, PROBST & WHITE, 1929

It must have been astonishing. A massive capitalist parade in the heart of Chicago, viewed by a flabbergasted sidewalk crowd roped off from the street.

A troop of express guards shielded by no fewer than one hundred police officers, some on horseback, advanced up the center of La Salle Street, a.k.a. the "Wall Street of the West." At the head of the caravan were Chief of Detectives John Egan and Deputy Commissioner of Police John P. Stege. Accompanying them was a flotilla of moving vans and armored trucks stuffed with cash.

When a business relocated in the 1920s, it was not a trivial undertaking. Office furniture had to be moved, along with equipment of all sorts and umpteen boxes of records and files and books. But when a bank moved, even more was involved—money in chests, sacks, and miniature safes also had to be relocated, which explains the regiment that inched up the famous thoroughfare on December 14, 1929. The officers of the Foreman State National Bank were moving into their new Art Deco home at 33 North La Salle Street, and they were bringing more than a billion dollars in cash and securities.

The Foreman State National Bank building used the most up-to-date elevators, as the Westinghouse Electric Elevator Company was proud to advertise. Author's collection.

Opposite: The entryway of the Foreman State National Bank in the 1930s, with its elaborate decoration over the door. Author's collection.

Some four years before, the Foreman Bank had purchased for $3.5 million an aging skyscraper, the historic Chamber of Commerce Building at the southeast corner of Washington and La Salle Streets. The site was especially desirable because it had alleys on two sides, which meant all four sides of the building were exposed to the sun (which is still the case). Oscar G. Foreman, chairman of the board, said, "We felt that because our institution is making such rapid strides and it's constantly becoming more difficult to secure a suitable banking location, that we couldn't postpone any longer the selection of a site to which we could move, or on which we could erect a fine structure for our purposes, should it become necessary."[1]

It didn't take long to become necessary. In March 1928, the bank announced it would indeed be erecting a new headquarters on the recently purchased site. It would be, at precisely 479 feet, 3 inches, the tallest bank in Chicago, they said. As an executive told the *Chicago Tribune*, "One of Chicago's oldest banks

33
NORTH
LASALLE

Lobby of the Foreman State National Bank building. Note the Art Deco mailbox. Photograph by the author.

enters a new era of development with the beginning of the new Foreman National Bank Building. Without the aid of consolidation the Foreman banks have grown to be one of the largest in Chicago, having over $100,000,000 in resources. . . . With the beginning of its new building the bank indicates the desire to keep abreast of the growth and expansion of Chicago." A month later the Bosley Wrecking Company began tearing down the Chamber of Commerce Building. On the day the new tower opened in December 1929, some one hundred thousand people flocked inside. As *The Chicagoan* put it, "buds & blooms filled the marble corridors with gorgeous tints, spicy exhalations. Coupon-clipping dowagers, weazened [*sic*] millionaires came to admire, murmured congratulations, sped to the tessellated roof, and there viewed another vast edifice, the Stock Exchange, rising to salute the North Star."[2]

The commission for the Foreman National Bank Building went to the prestigious firm of Graham, Anderson, Probst & White (GAPW), architects of the Civic Opera House, which opened only five weeks before the Foreman. The designer of the Foreman was Charles Beersman. The tower has been called an example of "stripped classicism." As with most other Chicago Art Deco skyscrapers, the building has an Indiana limestone tower and a granite base, though it uses a granite with "an unusual palest blue tint with black flecking that looks like spatters from a fountain pen," rather than the typical black granite.[3] This attractive blue stone, once called "Ausable Blue" and better known today as "Lake Placid Blue," is quarried in the Adirondack Mountains and remains popular for building materials, landscaping, and countertops. It is said to be particularly suitable for carving, which is borne out by the elaborate design cut into the stone above the impressive three-story entrance door on La Salle Street, which is similar to the entrance next door at One North La Salle. (These two skyscrapers occupy the entire block, making it an Art Deco showcase.) Art Deco aficionados will note that this botanical fantasy isn't typical of the "moderne" style of the 1920s, which leaned more toward geometric designs or stylized human and animal figures. Perhaps the designers took their cue from Chicago's pioneering architect Louis Sullivan, who was fond of vegetal motifs. In any case, although the overdoor might not be strictly Art Deco, it's one of the most impressive exterior decorative carvings in the city.

A contemporary guidebook called the building "a pretentious structure."[4] It consists of a thirty-eight-story (479-foot) central tower with two flanking twenty-two-story wings. The central tower is set back at the thirty-third floor and culminates in a tapered roof. The single-story first floor is for retail;

The original banking room of the Foreman State National Bank. Author's collection.

above is an impressive set of recessed three-story windows. As the *AIA Guide to Chicago* puts it, "The upward thrust is enhanced by recessed spandrels on the central portion of each façade in a darker terra-cotta than the piers."[5] The uniformity of the facade is thus cleverly rendered much more appealing than a flat surface. The lobby walls are dark green marble, and the chevron and angular motifs of the metalwork are Art Deco staples. The elevator doors, like the entryway overdoor, might not scream Art Deco, but they are glorious, and it's hard to conceive of them being designed outside the Jazz Age.

The bank's roots went back to 1862, when the institution was founded by Gerhard Foreman, an immigrant from Germany who settled in Chicago in 1857 and married a woman whose family was already in the lending business. The burning of the Foreman Bank's building in the Great Fire of 1871 was only a temporary setback. After Gerhard retired in 1885, his sons, the most prominent of which was Oscar G. Foreman, took over. By the spring of 1928, when the Foremans announced they would replace the old Chamber of Commerce Building with a skyscraper, everything looked positively rosy. And yet . . .

On October 28, 1929, a date forever known as "Black Monday," the Dow Jones Industrial Average dropped almost 13 percent, and the next day it fell another 12 percent. In the one month before the opening of the Foreman National Bank Building in December, the Dow lost nearly half its value. It was not a good time for a bank. Businesses that had secured loans from the Foreman Bank began to close, leaving their debts unpaid. Nervous depositors, fearful of a bank failure, started to withdraw their money. The Foreman Bank found relief in a merger with the State Bank of Chicago. Many Chicago Art Deco skyscrapers underwent name changes over the years, but this one changed after just a few weeks. The Foreman National Bank Building became the Foreman State National Bank Building—but at least the new bank was one of the three largest in Chicago.

Nevertheless, as the Great Depression continued to grind down the economy, Foreman State remained in shaky circumstances. A major problem was that Foreman State National Bank owned smaller, weaker

This spread: Art Deco ornamentation on the Foreman State National Bank building. Photograph by Ian McClellan.

banks outside of downtown Chicago. By June 1931 serious fears of a bank run arose, and Melvin A. Traylor, president of Chicago's First National Bank, summoned a bankers' meeting at his home. He agreed to guarantee Foreman State's deposits, but only if he assumed ownership. According to *Fortune* magazine, "the bank was indeed doomed." And it added: "The Foreman Bank was the last large Jewish bank within Chicago. Its collapse was not only a great blow to the pride of the Foreman family and their allies; it also dealt a great blow to the pride of Chicago Jewry."[6] The Foremans also lost their new skyscraper, which was taken over by the small American National Bank and Trust Company and renamed the American Bank Building.

The Foreman State National Bank's assets now had to be transferred to the First National Bank. And that meant—that's right—another currency caravan through the Loop. On the evening of June 8, 1931, with thousands of spectators again watching, more than three hundred police officers and security guards safeguarded the transfer of some $200 million of Foreman holdings to the headquarters of the First National Bank at Dearborn and Monroe Streets. The only things left in the Foreman State National Bank Building were the safety deposit vaults. Just before the money march, nervous depositors packed into the lobby. Walter W. Head, president of the bank, twice climbed on a chair to reassure the anxious assembly that their deposits were safe and the First National Bank would guarantee them. "Now," he cried, "all of you who believe me, raise your hands." After hands were lifted, he said, "All right then. All of you who aren't afraid get out of the way and let those who are afraid get up to the windows and get their money." Withdrawals were few and some clients even made deposits. But the headline in the *Chicago Tribune* broadcast the sad truth: "Foreman Bank Ends 69 Years Career in City."

STUDENT

No. 11

BUCKINGHAM BUILDING

HOLABIRD & ROOT, 1930

When the Buckingham Building at 59 East Van Buren Street was ready to accept tenants, it was advertised as "Just a step to Michigan Ave." The building to the east (separated by a narrow alley) is the Chicago Club, on the corner of Michigan Avenue and Van Buren. Because the Chicago Club is just ten stories high, the twenty-seven-story Buckingham Building rises above it and is therefore considered part of what architecture critics call the Michigan Avenue streetwall, a twelve-block stretch of historic buildings that face Grant Park.[1] A 1933 guidebook to Chicago called this row of structures "the best in skyscraper architecture from the days of its infancy to the present."[2]

The building's location was exceedingly desirable. In another newspaper ad, the rental agents proudly listed over a dozen firms that had taken space in the new tower, among them Charles Scribner's Sons, the American Railway Association, Vacuum Oil, the Religious Education Association, Amalgamated Roofing, and Industrial Publications. About a month later, the National Association of Real Estate Boards announced it was moving its headquarters into the Buckingham.

The developers of the Buckingham Building considered its proximity to Michigan Avenue a selling point. Author's collection.

It would be logical to assume the name of the Buckingham Building is related to the splendid Clarence F. Buckingham Memorial Fountain in nearby Grant Park, one of the largest fountains in the world, which opened to great acclaim in the spring of 1927. Some have argued that this was not the case, pointing out that the new skyscraper was initially known as the New Athenaeum, as it was replacing an 1886 building named the Athenaeum. However, the name "Buckingham" replaced "New Athenaeum" less than a year after the building's completion, and it's hard to believe the name change was not referencing the fountain, which could be seen from the skyscraper's windows and bore a name that brought prestige to the new tower.

In any case, the building was renamed again in 1940. The Socony-Vacuum Company of New York had been occupying four floors of the skyscraper since 1936, and when it signed a new ten-year lease, the owners agreed to call it the Socony-Vacuum Building, a name it retained until recently. Today, the building is known simply as the Buckingham.

The architects were Holabird & Root, a firm that was on a roll. In the two previous years they had completed 333 North Michigan, the Chicago Motor Club building, the Palmolive Building, and the Chicago Daily News Building, four skyscrapers that stand as Art Deco treasures to this day. In 1930, the year the Buckingham was finished, they also completed the La Salle-Wacker Building and the Chicago Board of Trade Building. For the Buckingham, they used a base of granite and a lighter colored tower of what's known as Milwaukee cream brick, made from Wisconsin clay that gave Milwaukee the nickname "Cream City." The facade is divided into five bays—four storefronts and the entranceway. What stands out in the Buckingham Building's facade is the vast span of granite, which covers nearly all of the first three floors (the granite is stepped in at the third floor)—an impressive and uncommon display.

The entrance door is unusually placed at the extreme right (west) of the facade, and the other bays are storefronts framed in dentillated aluminum, or aluminum strips with evenly spaced decorative notches. Above the large storefront windows on both the first and second floors are decorative panels with a treelike design. Various Art Deco ornamental motifs decorate the facade: Spandrels above and beneath the windows bear a terra-cotta plant design that the report from the National Register of Historic Places

describes as "a centered low-relief stylized design consisting of horizontal lily flowers and drooping leaves over an inverted papyrus."[3] The design might strike a viewer as confusing; the National Register speculates, "Perhaps these panels were installed upside down," which does seem to be a possibility, although it's difficult to think that the architects would have permitted such an oversight. Terra-cotta panels with keystone designs are on the twenty-fifth floor, and a large floral panel is above the entryway.

The Buckingham has an impressively large granite base. The entrance door is unusually placed at the extreme right of the facade. The tower itself is made of Milwaukee cream brick. Photograph by Andrea Blatz.

The twenty-seven-story building is nearly a square at ninety-two by ninety-eight feet; a notch is cut into the southeast corner that gives it something of an "L" shape, although it's barely visible from the street. Today, a large mural is on the west wall, part of an initiative called the Wabash Arts Corridor, which is billed as a "living urban canvas." Launched in 2013 by Columbia College Chicago, this project features an ever-expanding array of murals on various buildings in the South Loop. The current Buckingham mural is by an Italian artist who goes by Never 2501 and who has painted murals around the world. The mural is possible only because this portion of the west facade has no windows below the eighth floor. When the Buckingham was built, a building stood in what is now a parking lot and windows weren't needed or desirable.

The lobby has twenty-foot ceilings and has retained almost all its original Art Deco ornamentation, although the original ceiling light has been replaced with a fluorescent fixture. (The retail shops,

Is the Art Deco ornament upside down? Some observers think so. Photograph by Ian McClellan.

The elevator doors in the Buckingham Building display playful Art Deco renditions of forms of transportation. Photographs by the author.

however, have experienced considerable changes.) Of note are the brushed aluminum elevator doors, which are decorated with whimsical reliefs depicting modes of transportation—a locomotive, an airplane, a ship, and a balloon. According to the National Register of Historic Places, "Various features of the lobby are similar to that of the Chicago Board of Trade, which utilizes the same combination of grayish Notre Dame and Belgian black marble, open metal stair rail, stainless steel elevator doors, and the use of chevron designs in decorative stainless steel features." On the right as a visitor enters the lobby is a staircase featuring an Art Deco–styled banister.

In 1954 the building was sold for a reported $2.35 million to W. V. Carroll of the La Salle Street firm of Rodman & Linn, which was said to have "represented eastern interests in the transaction." Gradually, this area of Chicago was quietly turning into one of the great college towns of the world and the demand for student housing increased. In 2009 researchers at DePaul University issued a study that counted twenty-five educational institutions in the Loop and South Loop with over fifty thousand students. It made sense that the owners of the Buckingham would take advantage of this trend. In 2007 a group of investors turned it into a student housing facility with apartments ranging from studios to four-bedroom units and advertised "20 + schools within one mile."

ONLY
BUS
CTA

№. 12

LA SALLE-WACKER BUILDING

HOLABIRD & ROOT WITH ASSOCIATE ARCHITECTS REBORI, WENTWORTH, DEWEY & MCCORMICK, 1930

The look of the La Salle-Wacker Building when it was announced was different from what it became. At first it was to be a slender tower, with the wide facade (110 feet) on La Salle Street and the narrow facade (61 feet) on Wacker Drive. At 427 feet high, it was to have thirty-six rentable floors with a thirty-seventh-floor penthouse sheltering elevator equipment and the like. Some nine months later, an entirely new rendering was released. The developers had acquired the L-shaped lot that wrapped around the site. Now the building would be forty-one stories high and the facade on Wacker Drive would be 140 feet wide, more than double the original plan. Real estate editor Al Chase of the *Chicago Tribune* made much of the fact that the lot on the northwest corner of the site, which sold for $1.25 in 1837, was now valued at $4,536,983. He also added the extraordinary detail that a single family had owned the property for ninety-three years. Philip F. W. Peck, one of the stockholders and directors of the La Salle-Wacker Building Corporation, was the grandson of the man who had originally bought the lot nearly a century before.[1]

The powerful beacon atop the La Salle-Wacker Building was known as the "Sun Flash." It was said that pilots could see it two hundred miles away. A reporter described it as "a gigantic colored flower." Author's collection.

Unlike the Board of Trade Building with its pinnacle, sculptures, and aluminum statue of Ceres, the La Salle-Wacker Building, though handsome with its "stripped-down classicism and elegant setbacks,"[2] is not assertive or flamboyant. "Here is seen structural logic in its simplest terms," said the *Chicago Tribune* in 1931.[3] Logical, however, does not mean dull. The facade is ingeniously varied, with deep setbacks and vertical dark window rows with ornamental spandrels that emphasize verticality. Above the three-story granite base rises an H-shaped tower of Indiana limestone with projecting wings not unlike the Board of Trade Building. Above the twenty-fourth floor, the setback tower rises without interruption, but its projecting piers alleviate any possible monotony. The recessed rows at the very center of the facade rise interruptedly (and dramatically) from the base to the top. These architectural effects were highlighted because the building, like some others in Chicago (the Wrigley Building, the Merchandise Mart, the Palmolive Building), was bathed in floodlights, "so that the recessed bays," in the words of architectural historian Mark J. Bouman, "were illuminated, creating a vertical rhythm of light and dark at the top of the structure."[4]

The La Salle-Wacker Building had a beacon that, it was said, pilots could see two hundred miles away. Called the Sun Flash, it was first illuminated on August 29, 1930, a mere two days after the lighting of the beacon on the Palmolive Building. A reporter who witnessed its debut wrote, "A combination of the light of sixteen red neon tubes bisected by the glare from eight 8,000,000 candle power lamps, the effect of the Sun Flash beacon was bizarre. The eight fingers of white light seemed to shoot out from a crimson base, the whole appearing as a gigantic colored flower growing from the modernistic top of the building."[5] The white lights flashed in pairs, which gave the illusion that the beacon rotated, even though it was stationary. The beacon was sheathed in a system of mirrors that caused it to shine from reflected sunlight so that it glowed both day and night.

The virtues of the La Salle-Wacker Building were trumpeted in an advertisement in the *Chicago Tribune*:

> Most modern of all Chicago buildings, its elevators will be the fastest in the world, its office spaces the most scientifically planned for 100% usability, its inside parking space for your car an amazing convenience. Day-long daylight and fresh air are perpetually guaranteed by its fortunate surroundings—Haddock Court, widened La Salle Street, Wacker Drive and the River. The maximum distance from any desk to nearest window will be

27 feet. There is no dark inside court. . . . But a step to all forms of transit, yet no elevated, surface car, bus or locomotive rumbles by its doors. Here you can telephone and THINK in peace and quiet.[6]

Although the elevators might not have been the fastest in the world, they moved at a speed of one thousand feet per minute and were the fastest in Chicago. The rental agent said, "the plague of noisy, crashing elevator doors, which mars the quiet of a good portion of our skyscrapers, even some of the newest, will not be present in the La Salle-Wacker building. All doors will close automatically and noiselessly."[7] The elevator cabs were equipped with ventilator openings at the base and sides so that incoming air could alleviate any possible pressure on the eardrums caused by the high speed.

The La Salle-Wacker Building was unusual in that it was formally the work of not one, but two, architectural firms working in collaboration: Holabird & Root and Rebori, Wentworth, Dewey & McCormick. However, several sources agree that it was Andrew Nicholas Rebori who designed the La Salle-Wacker Building as well as its beacon. Rebori, a fascinating and forgotten figure of Chicago history, was born on the Lower East Side of Manhattan in 1886. His Italian-born father, an engineer, died in an accident when Andrew was only three and he grew up in poverty. Andrew used to go swimming in the East River with a childhood pal, Alfred E. Smith, who went on to become a four-time governor of New York and the Democratic candidate for president in 1928. Rebori worked at odd jobs in his teens while also making blueprints for some architectural firms and attending night school. He was admitted to the Massachusetts Institute of Technology and received a scholarship that enabled him to study architecture at the École des Beaux-Arts in Paris and the American Academy in Rome.

Rebori came to Chicago when he secured a teaching position at the Armour Institute of Technology. He had grand visions of beautifying Chicago. Once he ran into Daniel Burnham at the Cliff Dwellers Club and mentioned he was drawing sketches for a revamped Windy City. "That's right," replied the great man. "You stir 'em out of the bushes and I'll get 'em in the open."[8] In the early 1920s he cofounded the firm of Rebori, Wentworth, Dewey & McCormick. Leander McCormick, a member of the wealthy and influential family that owned the *Chicago Tribune* and the McCormick

The newly built La Salle-Wacker Building was advertised as standing at "The Gateway to Finance," which was an apt description. Author's collection.

Harvesting Machine Company, secured commissions to build for Chicago's elite.

Rebori's most arresting modernistic buildings were the Art Deco Madonna Della Strada Chapel at Loyola University and the Fisher Studio Houses, which he designed in collaboration with the multitalented artist Edgar Miller (see chapter 1). Rebori also designed the risqué "Streets of Paris" exhibition for Chicago's second World's Fair, the 1933–1934 Century of Progress Exposition. This exhibition was the showcase for the sexy fan dancer Sally Rand, the most famous name connected with the fair, and it is said that Rebori auditioned Sally on the rooftop of the La Salle-Wacker Building, most likely because that's where his office was.

After the opening of the tower, Rebori and his firm took the entire fortieth floor. Rebori appears to have been especially proud of the La Salle-Wacker lobby; for *Architectural Forum*, he wrote a long essay about it titled "A Lobby of Metal and Glass." Vertical strips of glass alternated with bands of metal:

> A chrome-nickel steel, Allegheny metal, was used as a wall surface, as base and cornice, and as the ceiling in the elevator lobby alcoves. . . . The highly polished surface counts as bright silver in contrast with the blue steel-like finish of the glass sheets. The lighting is in the form of an indirect polished metal trough carried continuously around the main lobby ceiling about 18 inches from the side walls.
>
> The elevator cabs are of all metal design. A two-foot, fluted band of highly polished aluminum runs vertically at the side walls, and continues across the ceiling of the cars, in a striking contrast with the pale blue enameled metal walls and light yellow enameled ceiling of the cab. . . . The vertically fluted panel above the elevator door is of monel metal. The elevator lobby floor has arrows and lettering as part of the terrazzo floor pattern, giving definite directions from the entrance vestibule to the various banks of elevators.[9]

Allegheny metal, a type of stainless steel, was a product of the Allegheny Steel Company of Brackenridge, Pennsylvania, which touted the product for its silvery brightness, easy cleaning, and "unrusting, unstaining, untarnishing qualities" that made it easier to maintain than conventional marble. Photographs of the original lobby do show an effective contrast between silver metal and blue glass, and the effect must have been vivid.

Of Andrew Rebori, the similarly unpredictable architect Stanley Tigerman wrote, "People who go against the grain often go unnoticed, particularly in a city such as Chicago, which at the time Rebori was designing was still dominated by the Chicago School, both pre- and post-Mies. Because places like Chicago, out of their intellectual insecurities, latch onto something like that becomes a trend so quickly, people like Rebori don't become very well-known and are swept under the rug." Paul Gapp, architecture critic for the *Chicago Tribune*, similarly spoke of Rebori's "free-spiritedness, versatility and eclecticism," adding that he was "a powerhouse of a man, and from what I've heard he was a charmer, too. I wish I'd known him personally."[10] When Rebori died in 1966, *The New York Times* called him "the last of a generation of influential Chicago architects."

In 1986, the La Salle-Wacker Building was given a "facelift," and according to newspaper reports, the lobby underwent "expansion" and the dreaded "updating," which undoubtedly meant the purging of the mirrors and the Allegheny metal, which are no longer extant. It had to be done, explained a building executive, because "with all the development in the neighborhood [the building] has become a prime location."[11]

The La Salle-Wacker Building also has a claim to a critical role in American culture. It was there that in 1955 an entrepreneur named Ray Kroc rented an 800-square-foot office and launched the company that eventually became McDonald's. It's said that when the elevator operators got to his floor, they announced that visitors had reached "Hamburger Heaven."

December, 1930 THE ARCHITECTURAL FORUM 25

IT'S EASY TO CLEAN *the doors and entrance door frames from the lobby to the stores—for they're of Allegheny Metal.*

EVER BRILLIANT *Allegheny Metal . . . dark blue glass . . . Allegheny Metal . . . glass—on down the lobby, each in bands 16 inches wide by 14 feet high. Both are held in place by strips of Allegheny Metal an inch wide.*

method of cleaning keeps the La Salle-Wacker Building lobby bright and neat

IT'S a striking effect . . . quite modern . . . that you see here in the silvery bright strips of Allegheny Metal, set off by contrasting glass. You see the sparkle of a thousand reflections—tastefully held in check by the sober sheen of glass as dark as night. The lobby's alive—every inch.

And the effect is as permanent as time itself—thanks to Allegheny Metal . . . to its unrusting, unstaining, untarnishing qualities. Even sulphurous smoke from nearby trains leaves this alloy bright.

This lobby costs slightly less than the customary marble walls. Yet it has a lustre and a freshness that marble seldom gives without continuous and costly attention.

But—what attention does Allegheny Metal need? Very little. Because it withstands every kind of corrosion it meets. It does become soiled through contact—just like the glass beside it. Then it is cleaned as easily as the glass . . . the metal is bright.

Where else to use this alloy

Not alone in lobby decoration—but in dozens of other uses—is Allegheny Metal preferred. For many-storied pilasters on the Empire State Building, New York City. For elevator cabs in the Mariner Tower, Milwaukee. For all kinds of kitchen and laundry equipment.

It's not an all-purpose metal, but it does have a thousand uses. Many of these affect the architect . . . many appeal to his clients. It would be worth your while to write, inquiring how Allegheny Metal fits into your plans.

ALLEGHENY STEEL COMPANY

Brackenridge, Pa. . . . *Offices:* New York, Buffalo, Chicago, Cleveland, Detroit, St. Louis, Milwaukee, Los Angeles. *Warehouse Stocks:* Joseph T. Ryerson & Son, Inc.—Chicago, Cleveland, Milwaukee, St. Louis, Cincinnati, Detroit, Buffalo, Boston, Jersey City, Philadelphia. In Canada: Samuel & Benjamin, Ltd. Toronto.

ALLEGHENY METAL

Licensed by the Chemical Foundation, Inc., under basic patents No. 1,316,817 and No. 1,339,378

As seen in this advertisement, the La Salle-Wacker Building lobby featured Allegheny metal, a type of stainless steel that was prized for its silvery brightness, easy cleaning, and its "unrusting, unstaining, untarnishing qualities." Author's collection.

Nº. 13

TRUSTEES SYSTEM SERVICE BUILDING

THIELBAR & FUGARD, 1930

On either side of the grand staircase in the banking lobby of the Trustees System Service Building are two large bas-relief panels. One represents Thrift and depicts a thriving businessman, a beehive (a traditional symbol of constructive enterprise), and an owl (representing wisdom). The other panel depicts, amid thorns, a tattered and barefoot old man: Thriftlessness. The first panel bears the caption "Life Prospers the Thrifty," and the second declares "Life Punishes the Thriftless." These phrases may seem like platitudes, but they were the mission of the company that built this building.

The Trustees System Service Corporation was the creation of an entrepreneur named John Charles Corcoran, who was born in Wisconsin Rapids, Wisconsin, in 1883. He was working in real estate in Birmingham, Alabama, in 1914 when an idea came to him. He saw that men with property and collateral had no trouble securing bank loans, but honest workingmen with no assets were subject to the predations of "loan sharks and pawnbrokers." Corcoran called such an industrious and honest toiler "The Man Who Works" and envisioned a bank just for him. And the key to the

Contrasting allegorical figures representing Thrift and Thriftlessness flank the grand staircase of the Trustees System Service Building. Photograph by the author.

worker's success would be—you guessed it—Thrift. "To put the essence of it all in a single word, no better can be found than that fine word 'Thrift.' Under the banner of Thrift the workers of the world discount every old fear and undertake any new endeavor. . . . One of the greatest of these new means to Thrift is the co-operative Industrial Bank, such as has been established under the name Trustees System Service."[1] In less than two decades, Corcoran, who began with a one-room Birmingham office containing "a desk, a chair, and a big idea," had relocated to Chicago and was planning a magnificent Art Deco skyscraper to house his prospering endeavor.

As his architects he chose the team of Frederick Thielbar (1866–1941) and John Reed Fugard (1886–1968). Thielbar and Fugard had previously designed two prominent Chicago towers—the Jewelers Building (1926, in association with Giaver & Dinkelberg) and the McGraw-Hill Building (1929). For Corcoran's project they utilized the Art Deco styling they had employed in the McGraw-Hill Building and devised a twenty-story skyscraper with an eight-story tower topped by a ziggurat and crown. From the beginning, the tower was called the Trustees System Service Building. The editors at *The Greater Chicago Magazine* wrote that it was going to be called Two-O-One North Wells, but that name never caught on.

The tower rests on seventy-foot caissons that reach down to hardpan. Heating was supplied by Scotch marine boilers, which were commonly used on ships and were said to cut down on air pollution. Like most Chicago Art Deco skyscrapers, the Trustees System Service Building uses setbacks in the manner required by the city's ordinance of 1923. The twenty-story foundation structure, however, rises straight up from the street and the first setback is at the twenty-first story—the base of the eight-story tower, which itself features several setbacks that give it a stepped profile. The base is limestone, not granite, and the upper section uses terra-cotta ornament and face brick—dark red at the bottom and a lighter orange higher up, a progressive brightening of hue that was earlier used on Chicago's Wrigley Building. The Trustees System Service Building was exposed to sunlight on all four sides and was said to have "the largest window areas in Chicago."[2]

The editors at *The Greater Chicago Magazine* predicted that the new Trustees System Service Building would be called "Two-O-One North Wells," but it was not to be. Chicago History Museum. Chicago History Museum, ICHi-189090.

The first floor was shops and stores, floor two was the public banking area, floors three and four held the offices of Trustees System Service, and the floors above were rented to various tenants. Early on, the building attracted occupants from foreign nations and became known as "The Chicago Home of International Businesses." In addition to the consulates of Belgium, China, Cuba, the Dominican Republic, Greece, Honduras, Hungary, Italy, and Mexico, it also housed the Italian Chamber of Commerce and the National Railways of Mexico. Two radio stations broadcast from the building, and it was said that during the Prohibition era it was possible to get a stiff drink at the discreet twenty-third-floor Skyline Restaurant, which had a terrace for evening dances.

The side of the building on Lake Street has two entrances—the eastern leads to what is called the commercial lobby, the western to the banking lobby—and another entrance is on Wells Street. The commercial lobby entryway is one of the building's (and the Loop's) greatest features. The door is set nearly six feet back from the facade, leaving ample room for a surround of ten Art Deco limestone panels created by the sculpture team of Eugene Van Breeman Lux and his wife Gwen Lux, who also did the window spandrels and the interior panels of Thrift and Thriftlessness. Based on themes of banking and business, the plaques have such forthright pro-business titles as "Credit Moves the Modern Business World," "To Safeguard Wealth Men Created Banks," and "Exchange by Barter Marked the Dawn of Trade."

Before this project, when Gwen Lux was all of

TRUSTEES SYSTEM
FOUNDED SERVICE MCMXIV
182

Opposite: The impressive entryway of the Trustees System Service Building. Photograph by Ian McClellan.

Above: A decorative panel by sculptor Eugene Van Breeman Lux and his wife, Gwen Lux, shows how the activities of stockbrokers encompass the globe. Photograph by the author.

twenty years old, the Luxes supplied panels for Chicago's McGraw-Hill Building. That building has since been demolished, although the facade bearing the Lux designs has mercifully been preserved. Eugene and Gwen (who was the more talented of the pair) eventually went their separate ways, divorcing in 1942. He kindheartedly acknowledged her superiority and went into industrial design, but she married twice more and continued her long sculptural career until her death in 1986. Some of her commissions include a statue of Eve for Radio City Music Hall in Manhattan and a large abstract sculpture for Wingate High School in Brooklyn, New York. Architects with whom she collaborated included Edward Durell Stone and Eero Saarinen. In January 1933, an exhibit of her works, including *Eve*, was held in New York, and a reviewer opined, "Gwen Lux's work is, in the main, of a decorative sort and some of it is very effective. . . . Much of the work shown attains fulfillment in shapes verging upon or approximating the abstract."[3]

Surrounding the door to the banking lobby is an extraordinary feat of cut-lead grillwork by Chicago artist Edgar Miller, who in his time was called "the most versatile artist in the United States." The grilles depict laborers carrying out various essential feats of work—mining, farming, logging, and so on. Miller, it might be said, has depicted "The Man Who Works," the intended patron of Trustees System Service.

Aficionados of marble will appreciate the interior's fulgurant shades of the stone—red, green, gray, and gold. An article from 1930 in the *Chicago Evening Post* said,

The check desk in the banking lobby of the Trustees System Service Building in 1931. The room boasted an impressive display of marble, and a contemporary journal called it a "symphony in stone." The building has two lobbies, the other being the commercial lobby. Author's collection.

> The romance of ancient Rome, with its mighty legions, and the Sahara Desert, with its burnoosed Arabs, lingers about the warm-toned red Numidian marble in the lobby of the Trustees System national headquarters, for this marble came from the old Roman quarries in northern Africa, and was used exclusively in the great palaces of the Imperial City. For centuries after the fall of the Roman Empire the quarries were lost, and it was not until late in the nineteenth century that they were rediscovered. It is said the Trustees System headquarters, the Carnegie Library in Pittsburgh and the Union Trust Company in Detroit are the only buildings in America which are fortunate enough to possess this rare relic of old Roman splendor.[4]

A year later, a piece in the marble trade magazine *Through the Ages* called the lobby a "symphony in stone."[5] Besides the red Numidian, other marbles on display include Tennessee marble, travertine, and dark green verde antico, which is used on the imposing staircase to the second floor.

It's common to begin to perceive buildings that are around thirty years old as old-fashioned, despite their aesthetic merit. "Modernizers" decide renovations are necessary to attract tenants. That process occurred in 1967 in the Trustees System Service Building, where the ceilings in the banking and commercial lobbies were lowered and covered with tiles, but fortunately, most of the alterations were done only on upper floors. On the second floor, Lux-designed plaques illustrating industrial finance were removed, along with gold-leaf trim, marble floors and walls, and decorative moldings. Most of the alterations to the Lake Street lobbies were reversed in the early 1990s.

Corcoran had good reason to be proud of his new skyscraper, but sadly, he did not enjoy his triumph for long. The Trustees System Service Building was still under construction in October 1929 when the stock market crashed and the Great Depression was on. The business of the company was providing loans for working people, and when those people lost their jobs, repayment became either difficult or impossible. In January 1934 a federal judge adjudicated the corporation bankrupt. The assets were found to be some $2.5 million less than the liabilities.[6]

This spread: The Trustees System Service Building has an impressively large creation of cut-lead grillwork by Chicago artist Edgar Miller. The subject might be called "The Man Who Works." Photographs by the author.

In 1949 the skyscraper was purchased by the Corn Products Refining Company, and the building became known as the Corn Products Building.[7] Six years later it was sold again and became the Chicago Tower Building. In 1998 the realty company American Invsco carried out a $30 million renovation and converted the tower into rental apartments and luxury corporate suites. Eight years later the company converted it into a 293-unit condo building under the name Century Tower. The entire iron roof ornamentation was removed by helicopter, cleaned, and reinstalled. In 2018, Golub & Company and USAA Real Estate bought the building for $60 million, upgraded it, and "deconverted" it back to apartments. This marked a notable trend in Chicago real estate dealings, as more and more agents were deciding that the condo conversion trend had peaked and greater profit was to be made by deconverting.

No. 14

ONE NORTH LA SALLE

VITZTHUM & BURNS, 1930

Employees who work in the One North La Salle building report that when they exit the elevators into the lobby they are regularly blocked by a group of people with their heads up and their necks swiveling. These visitors are taking part in a Chicago Art Deco walking tour, and they have just entered one of the greatest examples of the style.

When plans to erect the tower were announced, the *Chicago Tribune* said that not only was the new structure of maximal interest, but so was the building it was replacing. For standing on the lot and destined for demolition (along with three other buildings) was the historic 1889 Tacoma Building by Holabird & Roche, often cited as the world's first skyscraper. Whether that's true remains a topic of debate, but even so, it was a prestige building for the Windy City. (When it was torn down, pieces of the girders were given to various architects and contractors as mementos.) However, One North La Salle might be a rare example of a historic and preservation-worthy building being replaced by one even finer (though see chapter 20 for a similar case).

The lead partner of the architectural firm that

designed the tower, Vitzthum and Burns, was Karl M. Vitzthum (1880–1967), who was born in Munich, Germany, and studied at the Royal College of Building Technology before emigrating to America in 1902. Twelve years later he settled in Chicago and worked for some respected architectural enterprises, including GAPW, before forming a partnership with John J. Burns in 1919. Burns was born in New York City in 1886 and studied at Washington University in St. Louis. Biographical accounts of the architect usually mention that he was the father of nine.

The new company became something of a specialist in banks and built more than fifty throughout the Midwest, but they also designed some other major Chicago buildings, including the twenty-three-story Old Republic Building on Michigan Avenue (1924), the Home Bank and Trust Company in Wicker Park (1926), the Beaux-Arts Midland Club on Adams Street (1929), and the forty-five-story Steuben Club Building on Randolph Street (1929). One of their most dramatic buildings is St. Peter's Catholic Church on West Madison Street (1953), whose stark facade features an eighteen-foot-tall crucifix known as "Christ of the Loop." Fittingly, it's just around the corner from One North La Salle.

In August 1928 the *Chicago Tribune* said, "Following the vogue of using numbers for names, a Gold Coast method of nomenclature now spreading to the loop, this gigantic structure will be christened the 'No. 1 La Salle street building.'" A few months later it reported that construction crews were proceeding at the blistering pace of four stories per week.[1] Like several other Chicago Art Deco skyscrapers, One North La Salle is a limestone tower set upon a dark granite base. The limestone here is Indiana limestone, a ubiquitous building stone used in Chicago in the Art Deco era. The panels bordering the entryway are made of a special granite called Charcoal Black that is quarried in the environs of St. Cloud in central Minnesota and is some two billion years old.[2]

Like most other Art Deco towers in the city, One

The spectacular lobby of One North La Salle with its four-foot-high frosted glass and metal peacock light brackets is a regular stop on Art Deco tours of Chicago. Photograph by Andrea Blatz.

A sculptural panel depicts French explorer René-Robert Cavelier, Sieur de La Salle. Photograph by Ian McClellan.

North La Salle is set back as it rises—three stages in this case, with the central tower flanked by two side wings. The first setback is at the twenty-fourth floor, 265 feet above the sidewalk. Everything about the building emphasizes its verticality. The limestone piers separating the windows are plain and simple and rise in unbroken lines.

Architectural geologist Raymond Wiggers has remarked on the "elaborate decorative patterns" around the entryway and on the fifth floor, where a series of seventeen panels shows Native American chiefs, the allegorical figures of Atlas and Justice, and several explorers, including, of course, René-Robert Cavelier, Sieur de La Salle, the French adventurer who explored the Great Lakes region in the late seventeenth century and is said to have camped on the site of the building. On either side of the top of the entryway are two large figures representing Commerce and Transportation, and the doorway itself is banded by abstract Art Deco geometric motifs.

The sculptural work is by the French American sculptor Leon Hermant (1867–1936) and, Wiggers explains, shows "the amazing ability of this limestone to take intricate carving that still retains its details many decades later." Hermant came to the United States from France in 1903 to work on the French pavilion at the 1904 St. Louis World's Fair and remained, but he temporarily returned to his homeland to participate in World War I, even though he was nearing fifty. His obituary in *The New York Times* had a sad headline:

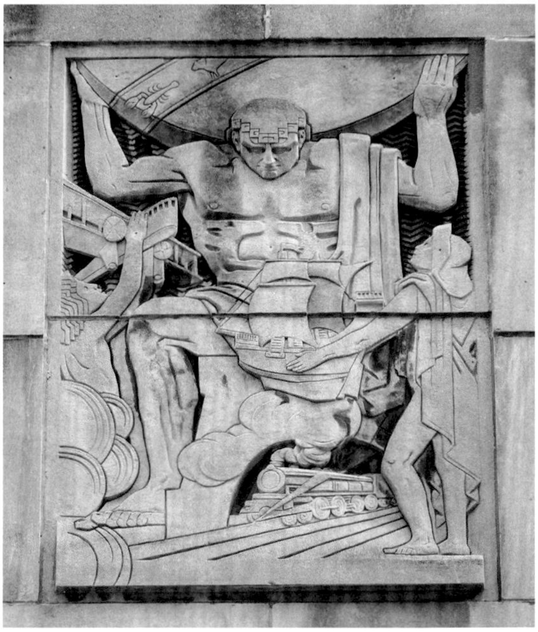

An allegorical representation of Atlas is one of seventeen decorative limestone panels surrounding the entryway of One North La Salle created by the French American sculptor Leon Hermant. Photograph by Ian McClellan.

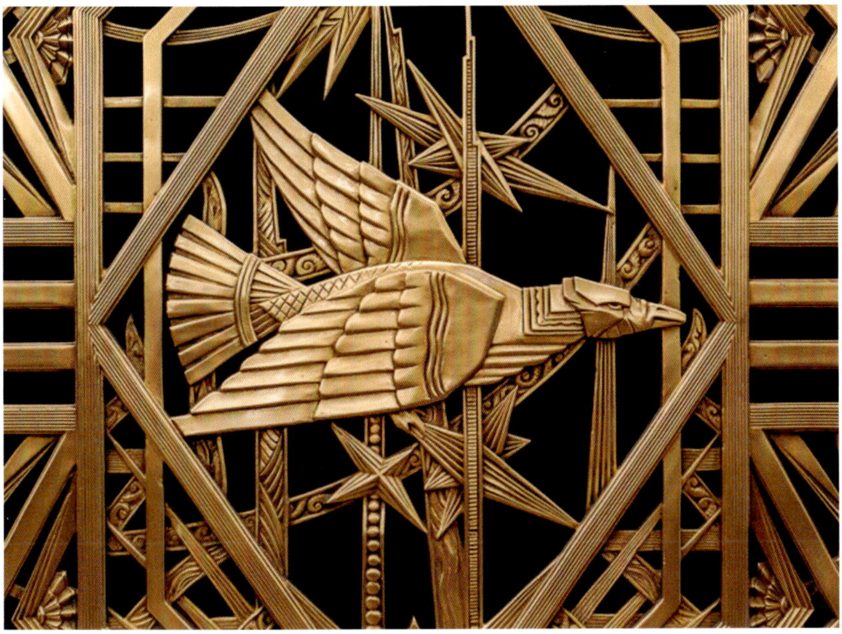

Stylized bird motifs are components of the Art Deco ornamentation of One North La Salle. Photograph by the author.

"French Sculptor Dies Alone in Room" (the police estimated he had been dead for thirty-six hours when found). Hermant completed many American projects in the first four decades of the twentieth century. Notable works of his in Chicago are two Michelangeloesque figures at the City Hall-County Building; the Louis Pasteur Memorial, which now stands in front of the restored Cook County Hospital; and an impressive Grecian frieze at the top of the MacLean Center on Michigan Avenue, which is so high up binoculars are needed to appreciate it.

The One North La Salle lobby is something of an Art Deco mini-museum with resplendent ornamentation throughout. Archetypal patterns, such as stylized chevrons, leaves, and birds (especially eagles), overlay the ceilings and the green-black marble walls. Meredith Taussig, the author of the Commission on Chicago Landmarks report on the building, has speculated that the lavish decorative scheme might owe something to Vitzthum's Bavarian background and that region's ornate Baroque and Rococo decorative stylings.

The most dramatic eagle is on the brass mailbox, a symbol of the words above it: "U.S. AIR MAIL." The grand frosted glass and metal light brackets that dominate the walls are Art Deco renderings of peacocks and make a strong impression. The prospectus for the building proudly emphasized this feature: "These brackets are 4 feet high and are hung 4 feet above the floor. The tail of the peacock on the bracket is fretted with green glass through which a dull light shines. The bright reflection of the bracket's main light is against the walls and ceiling, which gives a very charming and fetching beauty to the whole lobby." The gleaming bronze elevator doors feature low-relief half-dressed Grecian female figures symbolizing Success and Reputation. One observer said that these demoiselles "silently glide from closed to open and back again as in some primal Art Deco dance."[3]

One of the tower's most progressive features was its ventilation system, an early form of air-conditioning. The system operated only on the first eight floors, but in that space cold air was pumped in during the summer and warm air during the winter. It was felt that the first eight floors were the most crucial because of the noise factor. According to Al Chase, real estate editor at the *Chicago Tribune*, "The owners believe that this method will do considerably to reduce the ear strain caused by wailing taxicab brakes

The gleaming bronze elevator doors of One North La Salle feature Grecian female figures symbolizing Success and Reputation. Photograph by the author.

and the miscellaneous street uproar which supposedly blends into a soothing medley of sounds by the time it reaches the ninth floor. Anyway, from the ninth to the 47th, office tenants will have to yank up the windows in August if they get too warm."

Americans old enough to have grown up in a home without air-conditioning most likely remember first encountering it in the 1950s in a movie theater, but its history goes further back and Chicago architects were pioneers in the technology.[4] For example, Chicago architects Dankmar Adler and Louis Sullivan installed in their Auditorium Building of 1889 a mechanism that forced fresh air down a shaft where it was washed in a heavy spray cooled by crushed ice. The equipment moved more than twenty-five million cubic feet of air per hour. The forward-thinking Adler acknowledged, however, that true air-conditioning would require a refrigerant other than water. A decade later, architects William Le Baron Jenney and William Bryce Mundie designed an innovative system

Entryway to One North La Salle with Art Deco panels above. Photograph by Ian McClellan.

of forced ventilation for the Chicago National Bank Building (1899–1902). Although the apparatus did not actually dehumidify and cool the air, it managed to lower the interior temperature by eight degrees. Their design, according to historian Joseph M. Siry, "brought these mechanical arts to the cusp of air conditioning."[5] A Chicagoan named Samuel R. Lewis was president of the American Society of Heating, Refrigerating, and Air-Conditioning and the author in the early 1930s of an influential text titled *Air Conditioning for Comfort*. Chicago was also home to the Areologist Publishing Company, which issued several manuals on air-conditioning. One of their earliest books was *Air Conditioning Engineers' Handbook* (1931–1932).

Later, One North La Salle became the site of a couple of dark episodes. In September 1935 a young woman named Afton C. Ramsey, twenty-five, flung herself out a seventeenth-floor window and crashed on the sidewalk, barely missing several traumatized pedestrians. At the inquest it was learned that she had killed herself out of unrequited love for one John T. Janszen, who worked in the building as an assistant manager of an insurance company and had just become engaged to another woman. In October 1945 a gambler and former Rush Street speakeasy owner named Julius "Dollie" Weisberg shot and killed an Evanston automobile salesman named Joseph McKnight at the bar in the building's Regent Room. Weisberg was sentenced to die in the electric chair but mysteriously expired in his prison cell less than three days beforehand. The initial reported cause of death was a heart attack, but because Weisberg's demise was so conveniently timed, poison was suspected.

No. 15

CHICAGO BOARD OF TRADE BUILDING

HOLABIRD & ROOT, 1930

When, in 1928, developers announced the future construction of a new Chicago Board of Trade Building, reporter Philip Hampson of the *Chicago Tribune* was amused that a pit could be forty-four stories tall.[1] The headline: "Chicago's Pit Will Rise 600 Feet Over City." The building turned out to be much more than a pit—in the words of the Society of Architectural Historians, it is "one of the nation's most dramatically sited and beautifully conceived Art Deco office towers." The octagonal pit (eventually there were thirty) in which the physical trading was frantically carried out was indisputably the defining characteristic of the Chicago Board of Trade, and its silhouette became the building's logo.

One guide calls the building's lobby "one of the sleekest interiors of the 1920s anywhere. Expertly executed and dramatically lit, this space was the last word in up-to-date styling."[2] *The Chicagoan* magazine said shortly after its opening, "We believe the Board of Trade Building is the finest edifice of its kind, and of a good many other kinds, in the world. We unreservedly guarantee it to the visitor from afar, to the citizen of

Chicago and to the Iowa farmer."[3] The publication also joked, "La Salle Street has lost its place in the sun."

> The bright sunny days of olden times are gone—forever. The warm and kindly attentions of the sun will no longer minister to broker or customer. The banker refusing a loan will sit appropriately in the shadows, untouched by any mellowing light from the sun. These things, however, are not relics from the dark days of last November which even the sun in its mightiest efforts could not have brightened but are, instead, due to the towering heights of the new Board of Trade Building which stands directly south of the Street of Finance, rearing its majestic height against the sun.[4]

In the mid-nineteenth century the Midwestern prairies were being converted into agricultural land and Chicago's railroad network made it convenient for farmers to ship their products to the Windy City to be bought, stored, and delivered. The Chicago Board of Trade was established in 1848 to rationalize that shipping, selling, and storing; it also introduced a grading system for wheat. The year 1848 was such a pivotal moment for Chicago that it made the Board of Trade seem almost predestined: the Illinois and Michigan Canal was completed and the Galena and Union Railroad began operating, which were both useful for transporting grain and other products, and the city got its first telegraph, which the traders would make plentiful use of to do business throughout the nation. The Board of Trade became even more dynamic when it developed, in 1865, a system of "futures" that made it possible for a seller of grain to promise its delivery to a buyer at a certain date—the grain didn't have to change hands at the time it was sold. The system allowed risky, but potentially very profitable, speculation, and the pit was the scene of the action.

In 1848 trading took place in a room above the Gage and Haines flour market, but the enterprise grew relentlessly and inhabited eight successively larger spaces (none of which have survived) until 1885, when it moved into a ten-story skyscraper designed by the prominent architect W. W. Boyington, best known for Chicago's beloved Water Tower. That Board of Trade building became the tallest building in Chicago and the city's first commercial structure to use electric lights. It served the traders well until it, too, became too small and the exchange turned to the busy firm of Holabird & Root. At least six other

Opposite: The lobby of the Board of Trade Building has been called "one of the sleekest interiors of the 1920s anywhere." Photograph by Andrea Blatz.

Above: It's been suggested that the design of the Board of Trade Building was inspired by the drawing the American architect Bertram Goodhue submitted to the competition to design a tower for the *Chicago Tribune*. Like the Board of Trade Building, Goodhue's entry has stepped massing and a pyramidal roof with a statue on top. Author's collection.

architectural firms, including D. H. Burnham and Co. and Graham, Anderson, Probst & White, submitted designs or proposals, but Holabird & Root, who had been planning (at the board's request) a replacement building for about a decade, had the inside track.[5]

For the Board of Trade Building, Holabird & Root followed the formula they had used so successfully at 333 North Michigan and the Palmolive Building. The building features stepped massing—it's a classic limestone setback skyscraper of the Art Deco period that tapers as it rises. Unlike those two towers, however, it culminates in a pyramidal roof. This feature has led architect Stuart Cohen to conjecture an overlooked influence: the American architect Bertram Goodhue. Shortly before his death in 1924, Goodhue entered the celebrated competition to design a new tower for the *Chicago Tribune*. Goodhue's entry used stepped massing and featured a pyramidal roof with a statue on top.[6]

A 1933 guidebook, *All About Chicago*, recorded an entertaining anecdote about the completion of the frame of the Board of Trade Building:

> It has long been a custom of the construction workers to proudly raise the American flag aloft a completed steel skeleton, celebrating the occasion with whiskey supplied by the management. The custom has survived in spite of Prohibition. When the time came to raise the flag over the Board of Trade Building, Henry A. Rumsey, chairman of the building committee, was present with a hand movie camera and a galaxy of notables who had come to watch the ceremonies. The flag, however, failed to go up, because Mr. Rumsey, a dry, had declared that he would not supply the customary libations. There was a stalemate for twenty-four hours. But the flag was finally raised, when Mr. Rumsey announced that he had collected $2500 for the widows of two workmen killed during the construction, but that no further efforts would be made in their behalf unless the flag went up dry. He then passed out cigars, and the workers consented to the Volstead flag-raising.[7]

Holabird & Root's design not only gave ample space to the commodity exchanges but also included a much larger rentable area. At 605 feet high, the Chicago Board of Trade Building was Chicago's tallest building from 1930 until 1965, when the Chicago Civic Center, later renamed the Richard J. Daley Center, surpassed it at 648 feet.[8] It stands at the termination of what's been called the La Salle Street canyon, giving it one of the most dramatic and inescapable architectural sites in the Windy City—the throbbing financial heart of the metropolis.

To compare it to Holabird & Root's previous skyscrapers, 333 North Michigan and the Palmolive Building, is to appreciate how much variety of which the setback form was capable. According to architectural historian Richard Guy Wilson, "From the massive 9-story-tall base, large vertical sections rise, dominated at the center by a tower-like form. The façade is in a sense layered with the setbacks and rows of windows in vertical channels, which, through the depth and shadows produced, increase the sculptural impact of the building."[9] The emphasis on verticality, ingeniously achieved, is everywhere apparent. Vertical channels, setbacks, terraces, bays, projecting wings, and recessed spandrels darker than the surrounding limestone all create different patterns depending on the changing light, either from the sun or from artificial illumination.

The Board of Trade Building's Indiana limestone tower rests upon a base of a type of granite quarried near St. Cloud, Minnesota, known as "Cold Stone Pearl Pink." According to architectural geologist Raymond Wiggers, "In Chicago it's not the most common brand of St. Cloud to be seen, but it may very well be the most beautiful. From a few paces away its matrix of coarse crystals—black hornblende and biotite, glassy gray quartz, pink and white feldspars—resemble the colored dots of a pointillist painting. An essay in dynamic equilibrium, they create the pleasant illusion of maintaining overall stasis while vibrating slightly in Brownian motion."[10]The Art Deco ornamentation is ample but refined. Below the thirteen-foot-diameter clock at the top of the base are carved the words "Chicago Board of Trade," and on each side of the clock is a grain-related figure carved by Alvin W. Meyer, who also contributed a series of limestone bas-reliefs to the Chicago Daily News Building. On the left

The grand clock on the face of the Board of Trade Building is flanked by two sculptures representing figures in the history of grain—a Mesopotamian holding wheat and an American Indian holding corn. Photograph by Ian McClellan.

is a Babylonian holding wheat; on the right is a Native American holding corn. Above the clock is a stylized eagle, which Meyer explained as "emblematic of the spirit of America guarding our national interests."[11] The building was crowned by a popular observation platform on the thirty-fourth floor, which remained a tourist attraction into the 1970s, well after the building was replaced as Chicago's tallest. Another decorative touch by Meyer is a band of geometric and leaflike forms that runs just above the base. Wilson comments that these motifs appear to borrow from the celebrated 1925 exhibition in Paris.[12] The facade also features Art Deco renderings of grain, grain traders, and cattle.

As impressive as the building's appearance is, its effect is made greater by the highly unusual site facing a north–south thoroughfare. Chicago is planned on a fairly strict grid pattern, with blocks of equal size. But, as historian Edward Keegan has explained, "a shift in the grid at Jackson and LaSalle Streets produced the rare Chicago site where a building could sit within the city plan and have an axial relationship to the street it fronts."[13] The Board of Trade had, of course, occupied the site since Boyington's 1885 tower, which itself had created an epic grid barrier; now the effect became even more majestic.

A much-discussed feature of the Board of Trade Building is the thirty-one-foot-tall Alcoa aluminum statue atop the pyramidal roof. The figure, entitled *Ceres, Goddess of Grain and Harvest*, is by Chicago-born sculptor John Storrs, who worked in a modernistic abstract style influenced by cubism. Ceres, who holds a bag of grain in her right hand and a sheaf of wheat in her left, has no face, a feature that has been explained by the artist's belief that a face was superfluous because the statue was 609 feet above the street. Storrs couldn't conceive, the story goes, that one-hundred-story skyscrapers, from which one could look *down* on the statue, lay in the future. Yet cubist renderings of human figures sometimes have no faces, or only suggestions of faces (for example, Pablo Picasso's *Girl with a Mandolin* of 1910 and Constantin Brâncusi's *Head of a Woman* of 1925), and Storrs was in that tradition.

Also, at this time Art Deco designers were moving into the "streamlining" vogue, and *Ceres*'s gleaming aluminum surface uses one of the most prevalent streamlining materials. Sleekness, not detail, was all.

A "moderne" statue of Ceres, Roman goddess of grain, by John Storrs tops off the Board of Trade. Photograph by Ian McClellan.

In 1930, Philip Hampson interviewed Storrs, who explained his reasoning. The great height of the roof was a minor consideration, but modernism was a greater one and a true-to-life rendering was not:

> When I was given the order to execute a sculptural piece to top the Board of Trade building, I had two major points to consider. First I wanted my work to be in architectural harmony with the building on which it was to stand. Second, I wanted it to be symbolical of the business of the organization the structure was to house. The first point I have accomplished through treating the subject in an extremely modern manner. The vertical lines of the building itself are retained in the lines of the statue. Because of the great height at which it will stand the matter of detail did not have to be taken into consideration. The outline of a woman's figure is suggested rather than rendered exactly. As to the second point, I borrowed a thought from the classical period. . . . However, while the thought is classical, the treatment is entirely modern. From the street the statue will appear to pedestrians mostly in silhouette. The hands holding the sheaf of wheat and the sample bag extend from the body abruptly instead of being attached to arms. The face, too, is suggested, inasmuch as there are no regular features.[14]

Hampson especially praised the sculpture for its continuation of the modern lines of the skyscraper, a feature he found lacking in some other statues used as building decorations. Similarly, Oskar J. W. Hansen, writing in *The Chicagoan*, was well aware of Storrs's standing as a modern artist: "John Storrs is bringing sculpture back into its pristine unity with architecture. Sculpture has never thrived apart from the wall and the column. The feeling of monolithic severity which he so faithfully represents carries with it an atmosphere as serene as the snows of Mount Olympus."[15] "Monolithic severity" is an excellent description of the abstract *Ceres*. Finally, *Ceres* isn't the only statue at the top of the building. Just below Storrs's creation are much more realistic figures with faces—faces that presumably are also difficult, if not impossible, to see from the street.

Another oft-told story about *Ceres* has to do with its putative model, one Madelyn La Salle FioRito. Many respectable sources state that when she was all of fourteen years old, John Storrs discovered her in an elevator in the Fine Arts Building and asked her to pose for *Ceres*. This engaging story has been debunked by researcher Ed McDevitt, who consulted Storrs's diaries and found no mention of a model in general or FioRito specifically. In fact, the story that she modeled for *Ceres* was unknown until an interview with her in the *Chicago Tribune* in 1954. McDevitt also interviewed Storrs's granddaughter, who insisted that, although Storrs once did briefly meet FioRito, he used no model at all for the statue. Finally, Storrs's studio was in the Tree Studio Building, not the Fine Arts Building—though he spent nearly all his time in Paris, where he designed the sculpture.[16]

Ceres also inspired what must be one of the most groan-inducing puns in Chicago's literary history. Richard Atwater, writing in *The Chicagoan* magazine in 1930, expressed a wish that the statue should be mounted on some sort of turntable so that it could revolve. Then it would be a "Whirled Ceres."[17]

Holabird & Root had no less grandiose plans for the ground-floor, three-story arcade: "In this arcade will be found an expression indicative of the progressive spirit associated with the great mart known as the Board of Trade. . . . At the end of the arcade will be found a lighting system unique in the impressive vertical shafts of illuminated glass running from floor to ceiling with a burnished metal reflector, which will cast a silvery light over the entire area of the arcade."[18]

The three-story lobby, which is encircled by a balcony, reportedly contains seven types of marble. One of them is the so-called Batesville marble, which is in fact a type of limestone quarried in Arkansas. As explained in a 1932 report on the "black marbles" of Arkansas, "It is the commercial practice . . . to apply the name marble to all limestones which take a high polish."[19] In the Board of Trade Building lobby it's used for the floor pavers, and its ability to "take a high polish" gives the surface its luminous sheen. The lobby's majestic Art Deco decoration, with its tall black marble skyscraper-shaped piers that evoke an urban skyline, exudes dignity and confidence, worthy attributes for investors and speculators. The lighted panel that runs across the ceiling and down the wall to the balcony was publicized as the "world's largest light fixture." The wall lighting fixtures are behind multicolored translucent glass. Stairways and railings are brass and feature wheat motifs. Richard Atwater told of a trader who visited the new building: "He is much impressed by the palatial architecture of his impending home, the number of doorknobs alone in the new

It's understandable that visitors to the Board of Trade Building would interpret the decoration on the elevator doors as a martini glass, but it's a stylized plant motif. Photograph by the author.

The original trading room was the setting of the grand mural of Ceres by Chicago artist John Warner Norton (*above*). The restored mural is now in an adjacent atrium (*opposite*). Chicago Board of Trade Building (1930), Chicago, Illinois. Holabird and Root, architects. Historic Architecture and Landscape Image Collection, Ryerson and Burnham Art and Architecture Archives, The Art Institute of Chicago. Digital File # L031938 333. Photograph of restored mural by the author.

edifice just about taking his breath away. He isn't quite certain, however, about the new elevator doors, which he discovered done in contrasting colors, like an awning. He is sure it must be in good taste, but can't get over a slight fear that it isn't quite dignified."[20]

The original trading floor, where the pit was located (along with smaller neighbors), was above the ground-floor lobby; it was reported at the time that three thousand miles of electrical wire were laid beneath the trading floor.[21] The 115-by-165-foot trading floor initially had a ceiling 57 feet high and enormous windows. Relief sculptures by Meyer decorated the entry doors. The room was dominated by a mural of

Statues representing Agriculture (*above*) and Industry (*opposite*) salvaged from the 1885 Board of Trade Building now stand near the entrance on Jackson Boulevard. Photograph of agriculture statue by the author; photograph of industry statue by Ian McClellan.

Ceres that was 31 feet 6 inches tall and much more voluptuous than the roof statue. It was done by the prolific and important Chicago artist John Warner Norton.

Like some other Chicago Art Deco skyscrapers, the Board of Trade Building has endured changes, the most obvious being the addition of two respectful, if not exactly inspired, annexes—the south one, designed by Helmut Jahn, was built in 1982 and the one on the east, by Fujikawa Johnson and Associates, was added in 1997. In 1975 the original six-story-high trading room was sliced horizontally into two levels of three stories each and much of the room's original character was lost, including Norton's mural of Ceres. This treasure was later found. It had lost paint and been cut horizontally in two, but it was restored by Louis Pomerantz of the Art Institute of Chicago, mounted in a frame designed by Helmut Jahn, and placed in the atrium.[22]

In the early twenty-first century the building underwent a $22.6 million renovation by Chicago-based Harboe Architects, under the guidance of Austin/AECOM. The design team used vintage photographs to model the restoration, recreated missing light fixtures and nickel silver elements, and restored the lobby to its original splendor while also rehabilitating the exterior. In 2007 the Commission on Chicago Landmarks gave the project an award for Preservation Excellence.

An unexpected restoration occurred in 2005 when two lost statues were returned to the site. But these sculptures were not from the 1930 building. They were from the 1885 Board of Trade building! The Forest Preserve District of DuPage County had found the two twelve-foot-tall Greek female figures representing Agriculture and Industry lying in the grass at the former Glen Ellyn estate of Arthur Cutten, a one-time trader who salvaged them when the original building was demolished. Just in time for the building's seventy-fifth anniversary, the statues were prominently placed in a renovated plaza where, looking almost as good as new, they contemplate the passersby on Jackson Boulevard.

The statues might have returned, but the six-hundred-foot-tall pit that *Tribune* reporter Hampson joked about is gone—in fact, all the pits are gone. Beginning around 2006, computer trading systems gradually rendered them obsolete and then the COVID-19 pandemic of 2020, which severely discouraged face-to-face interaction, gave them the coup de grâce.

CERES
CAFE

No. 16

MUNDELEIN CENTER

NAIRNE W. FISHER & JOSEPH W. MCCARTHY, 1930

The great Art Deco skyscrapers of Chicago were almost exclusively built by major corporations and other capitalist enterprises. The Mundelein Center was built by nuns. They were a special group of nuns, who deserve the name later given them—"sister builders."[1] Their official name was the Sisters of Charity of the Blessed Virgin Mary, a.k.a. BVMs.

The BVMs were founded in Dublin in 1833 but within a decade had relocated to the United States, first to Philadelphia and then to Dubuque, Iowa. By the 1860s they were active in Chicago and in the last decade of the nineteenth century, they were operating the Seminary of the Sacred Heart, where they taught the daughters of Chicago's privileged classes while also providing tuition-free education to some one thousand girls from deprived areas. In 1899 they opened, in a rented three-story neighborhood building, St. Mary's, the first central Catholic high school for girls in the United States. Nationally, the BVMs numbered over two thousand (with more than three hundred sisters in Chicago), and they operated a college, five academies, thirty high schools, and over one hundred elementary schools.

The range of talents possessed by the BVM nuns is evident in this etching depicting the Mundelein Center by Sister Mary Carmelyn. Author's collection.

During the Art Deco period, the head of the order was a sharp Irish-born nun named Isabella Kane (1865–1935). When Father George Mundelein, Chicago's first Roman Catholic cardinal, expressed his wish to establish a Catholic women's college, he naturally turned to Mother Isabella. The conventional plan for a college would have been something like a grassy quadrangle surrounded by Colonial-style low-rise classrooms and dorm buildings. But that was not the vision of the forward-looking Isabella Kane. "Run up into the air," she said. "It is a novel idea that will attract girls—it is the modern way of living. Why not have the expanse go up instead of spreading. . . . The time is ripe."[2] It was going to be a "skyscraper college."

The energetic Mundelein envisioned the creation of a "Catholic University of the West" in the Windy City and advocated higher education for women, which was something of a novel concept but one that was becoming urgent with the growing demand for women religious to teach in Chicago's burgeoning parochial schools. But if there was to be a college for Catholic women, the nuns who taught them would themselves have to master university subjects such as foreign languages, mathematics, philosophy, education, science, and so on. The nation's Catholic universities were exclusively male, and the Jesuits opposed coeducation.[3] The Catholic establishment also frowned on Catholic women attending state universities. As a result, a major component of Mundelein's ambition was that a college for women was to be directed (and paid for) by the BVMs, who by this time had become a major educational force. As the cardinal explained at the time, "The need of a Catholic college for women is patent to everyone and becomes more urgent every day. More and more are women taking the places formerly occupied by men, in the professions, in business, in literature, in the shaping of public opinion, even in science. The time has come when they are receiving the advantages and the responsibilities of equal suffrage with men. It stands to reason then that we must provide equal educational advantages for our Catholic girls if we expect them to take front rank with the women of the future."[4] The cardinal was also egalitarian. His idea of a proper school was one "where girls of all classes meet on an equal footing, where the one aristocracy is the aristocracy of brains."

The cardinal discussed the project with the sisters as early as 1916, but they regretfully informed him they were in no position to undertake the fundraising and financial burden. The matter languished until the late 1920s, when Mundelein began pushing it again (it's said he was quite a pest). This time, the BVMs mortgaged their two high school buildings and got a loan of half a million dollars.

Thus the existence of the Mundelein Center is due to two individuals remarkably enlightened for the time. Cardinal Mundelein demonstrated a broad-minded attitude toward equal education for women of all social classes, and Mother Isabella showed the same progressivism regarding Art Deco architecture.

At first the sisters considered a Loop location but then decided to build in proximity to Loyola University, on Lake Michigan at the northern end of Chicago, and quickly purchased two lots just south of that campus. Cardinal Mundelein had a preferred architect, Joseph W. McCarthy, who was a former collaborator of Daniel Burnham and something of a specialist in Catholic buildings. He built twenty-nine churches in Chicagoland, among them Corpus Christi (1916), Our Lady of Peace (1919), and St. Philip Neri (1928).[5] He also designed the original Cathedral of St. Raymond Nonnatus in Joliet, Illinois (1918).

McCarthy's credentials were solid, but his first depiction of the building was in the Colonial style—sort of a bloated Independence Hall made of red brick—and not to Mother Isabella's liking. Because her vision had by now become imbued with the "moderne" spirit of the age, she called in Nairne W. Fisher, a progressive architect from Dubuque, where Mother Isabella had met him. Mother Isabella didn't want to alienate Cardinal Mundelein, so McCarthy remained on the team as supervising architect while Fisher was designated design architect. The construction crew broke ground just two days after the stock market crash helped launch the Great Depression in 1929. But the sisters kept going. The building was a blessing to the workers, who appreciated having jobs.

Joining Mother Isabella was a nun named Sister Justitia Coffey, who became the hands-on supervisor of construction. Every morning she would walk to the site accompanied by a novitiate and her collie, Prince. She regularly discussed the progress with William Lynch, the construction manager, as well as other workers, while securing the permits and construction supplies.[6] The skyscraper was built in a short eleven months. Considering that it was erected in a heavily Catholic city, we can assume that many of the workers were of that faith. One might think the constant presence of Sister Justitia and her colleagues invigorated their labors, and one would be correct. Construction manager Lynch said, "I was never driven harder than by these gentle women."[7] It was at the sisters' request that the new school was to be named Mundelein College. Sister Justitia became the first president.

According to historian Pauline Margaret Abraham Tarvardian, "Mundelein College opened its doors on 29 September 1930 with an enrollment of 384 students, 250 of whom were freshmen. . . . The original intention was to enroll only freshmen. Numerous petitions from priests moved the administration to accept a limited number of sophomores and juniors. Tuition was seventy-five dollars per semester."[8] A year after opening day, *Chicago Tribune* reporter James O'Donnell Bennett traveled uptown to see the new edifice.[9] He was enthralled by the ethnic diversity of the students: "American, English, Australian, Greek, Syrian, Italian, French, German, Irish, Polish, Czecho-Slovakian, and Hungarian. One comes from China and one from Porto Rico. Twelve are Greeks, among them a Penelope and an Andromache." (Ten percent were Protestant.)

He was further impressed by the building's size: "a stone structure that towers above the villas and residential hotels of the neighborhood . . . From the terrace on the eleventh floor you can on a clear day see the shores of Michigan." But what really struck him was not the skyscraper, but the sisters who built it. He called it "a mighty monument to the energy and originality of American womanhood." The sisters' days, he said, ran from 5 in the morning until 9:30 at night. He found them doing research in zoology and biology and teaching everything from music to languages to journalism to science to finance to physical education. They operated Dictaphones, mimeographs, "several types of computing machines," and even the elevators, all while carrying a debt with an interest of $90,000 a year. "But they are not apprehensive, nor do they repine," Bennett wrote. "Happier women . . . I never saw."

In recent years a BVM sister achieved national fame in an unexpected manner. She was Sister Jean Dolores Bertha Schmidt, a.k.a. "Sister Jean," who rocketed to stardom as the basketball chaplain and mascot of the Loyola University men's basketball team, which unexpectedly made it to the Final Four of the NCAA Tournament in 2018, when Sister Jean was ninety-nine years old. She was regularly seen on televised games in her maroon and gold scarf, providing motivation and prayers. Born in 1919, she was a decade older than the Mundelein Center.

Large sculptures representing the archangels Uriel and Jophiel flank the entryway. Photograph by Amerique, https://commons.wikimedia.org/wiki/File:Guardian_Angels,_Mundelein_Center,_Loyola_University_Chicago.JPG. CC BY 3.0, https://creativecommons.org/licenses/by/3.0/deed.en.

As a true "skyscraper college," the structure not only contained classrooms and a large auditorium but also featured living areas for the sisters, a kitchen capable of feeding one thousand diners, an indoor pool, a gymnasium, libraries, a bookstore, reception rooms, a theater, a radio broadcasting studio, laboratories, storage rooms, rehearsal rooms for orchestra and glee club, twenty music studios with twenty grand pianos, the marbled Art Deco Stella Maris chapel, and an exercise area on the rooftop suitable for tennis. The physics department appropriated an unused elevator shaft to install the world's longest Foucault pendulum (an apparatus that consists of a large swaying

The side door of the Mundelein Center bears the monogram BVM, for the name of the nuns' order, Sisters of Charity of the Blessed Virgin Mary, and their motto, *sicut lilium interspinas* ("find the lily among thorns"). Photograph by Warren LeMay. CC BY-SA 2.0, https://creativecommons.org/licenses/by-sa/2.0/deed.en.

object suspended from a cable that, by its movement, demonstrates the rotation of the earth). The Mundelein pendulum, which descended one hundred feet through nine floors of the building, was the inspiration of Sister Mary Therese Langerbeck, a professor and astrophysicist. The students also formed a debate team. Their first competition was against the men of nearby Loyola University and the topic was "Resolved: The emergence of women into public life is to be deplored." The Mundelein students, taking the negative side, won handily.[10]

A Jesuit priest named Edward J. Reynolds, in an article titled "Ivy and Rectangles," called the skyscraper "one of the finest conceptions in the new manner of set-back rectangular surfaces of stone, the bearer of a strange new beauty that in time will pass into novel and unhazarded beauties of mass and line."[11] The building is in the classic Chicago Art Deco mode, with a limestone surface and setbacks. The National Register of Historic Places calls it "a tripartite ziggurat with setbacks on the fourth, eighth, and eleventh stories." The recessed center of the facade accentuates the building's verticality.

The Indiana limestone is crowded with ancient shells that can be perceived with a magnifying glass. This particular limestone is renowned for its ability to handle intricate carving, and at the request of Mother Isabella, designer Charles Fisher (brother of the architect) devised four-story figures of the archangels Uriel and Jophiel that were then carved by sculptors from the North Shore Stone Company.[12] In one hand, Uriel holds the book of wisdom, and her other hand, raised, points to the cross fourteen floors above. Jophiel clutches the earthly globe (crowned by a cross) and the torch of knowledge.

The windows and entry doors are decorated with classic Art Deco geometric motifs; the grillwork features zigzags and rectangles. "BVM," the monogram of the sisters, is above the doors on the front and the sides. Prominent over the entryway is the BVM motto *sicut lilium interspinas* ("find the lily among thorns"), reflecting the flower associated with the Madonna; fittingly, the lily comprises a portion of the ornamental decoration. The abundance of Art Deco embellishment surprises aficionados of the style today; when the edifice was new, it screamed "moderne," just as Mother Isabella and Sister Justitia wanted.

The grand staircase of the Mundelein Center is the first thing a visitor sees upon entering the building. Courtesy of the Women and Leadership Archives, Loyola University Chicago.

An image of the Madonna is a fitting ornament on the exterior. Photograph by Ian McClellan.

Upon entering the main door, a visitor is confronted by the grand staircase. The stepped walls on its sides are adorned with the then-popular motif of three horizontal stripes, commonly referred to in Art Deco lingo as "speed lines." Both students and faculty were told not to use the steps; they were reserved for formal occasions like graduations (it was an ideal place to pose a large group). Similarly, the students were advised to use the elevators only if they were going above the fourth floor.

The walls and floors of the vestibule are covered with various hues of colored marble; the floors bear a theatrical diamond pattern and imposing vertical radiator screens bear a geometric rendering of the building's profile. The elevator doors reiterate the patterns on the exterior; their sunburst design represents another of the emblems of the BVMs. Some of the most characteristic Art Deco decor is to be found in the college's social rooms, with their diamond-patterned marble floors and (for the time) up-to-date lighting.

Many words of praise were given to the new building, but surely the most pleasing were those of Pope Pius XI. When shown photographs of the towering "skyscraper college," he said, "I don't know that it is the greatest college in the world, but I am sure it is the one nearest heaven."

Mundelein College went out of existence in 1991 when it merged with Loyola. Beginning in 2004, the structure underwent thorough renovation and is now known as the Mundelein Center for Fine and Performing Arts.

No. 17

MERCHANDISE MART

GRAHAM, ANDERSON PROBST & WHITE, 1930

If Chicago's enormous Merchandise Mart were built on a standard 125-by-150-foot lot, how tall would it have to be to contain its four million square feet? When the building was new, general superintendent Frank F. Sengstock did the math: more than 200 stories high—way more than the Burj Khalifa, currently the world's tallest skyscraper, which has 163.[1]

With its zigzags, arrows, chevrons, Mayan patterns, terrazzo triangles, elevator doors emblazoned with arcs and diagonals, elegant sconces, triangle-shaped brass stairway posts, gray limestone walls, chamfered corner turrets, stylish murals, and three-part facade, the Merchandise Mart is something of a catalog of Art Deco themes done by an architectural firm expert in the "moderne" aesthetic.

Yet it's possible that visitors, while impressed by the building's mighty bulk looming over the north bank of the Chicago River, especially when it's illuminated, might not be sure what it's for. The functions of most of the city's other Art Deco skyscrapers are clear—the Daily News Building held the offices and presses of a newspaper, the Carbide and Carbon Building and the Palmolive Building were the headquarters of major corporations, and the purposes of the Central Post Office, the Civic Opera House, the Board of Trade Building, and the Lawson House YMCA are obvious from their names. The Merchandise Mart obviously has something to do with merchandise, but what exactly?

It had to do with Marshall Field, a name that looms large in the history of Chicago. Today, most people encounter the name at the Field Museum, and the Field Building on South La Salle Street is one of Chicago's largest skyscrapers. But it was also the name of the legendary Marshall Field & Co. department store on State Street, which was acquired and renamed by Macy's in 2005. Just about any Chicagoan over a certain age has fond memories of the wonders to be found in its magical interior, especially at Christmas, when crowds of people mobbed the sidewalks to gape at the window displays.

Marshall Field (1834–1906) was born in Massachusetts, and at age twenty-one, like many an ambitious Northeastern lad, he moved to Chicago to make his fortune, which he did. He got a job at a wholesale business and soon was a partner in the firm of Farwell, Field, and Company. The new company then added Levi Leiter as a junior partner, and Farwell left to go into real estate. At the time, the reigning merchant prince in Chicago was Potter Palmer, but he wanted to slow down, so he sold his entire retail business to Field and Leiter. In 1868, the partners opened a store at the corner of State and Washington Streets, where Macy's is today. Three years later, it was destroyed in the Great Fire. The present building was completed in four stages between 1902 and 1914. After Field bought out Leiter in 1880, the business became Marshall Field & Co. and became the largest store in the world. It boasted a Tiffany glass dome, a bookstore, a medical dispensary, a nursery, a multilingual information desk, and meeting rooms for women's groups. The Walnut Room (1907) was the first full-service restaurant in a department store.

Field was not only in the retail business; he also sold merchandise wholesale—a great deal of merchandise. Field owned not only the world's largest store but also America's largest wholesale business. Field had a small army of "road agents" who spread out across the country in search of sellable goods, and the wares they purchased were stored in an eight-story, city-block-size warehouse at Adams and Franklin Streets that opened in 1887, a precursor to the much larger Merchandise Mart.

From 1923 to 1930 the president of the company was the energetic and confident James Simpson, who was born in Glasgow in 1874. His personality can be appreciated by knowing that when he asked Marshall Field for a raise—one year after being hired and making six dollars a week—Field replied that at Simpson's age, he was making only five dollars a week. "Well, Mr. Field," Simpson answered, "perhaps that is all you were worth." (He got the raise.) Simpson hoped the solution to competition was an even larger wholesale business.[2] And an even larger warehouse. How large? The biggest building in the world.

Simpson selected as his architects Graham, Anderson, Probst & White (GAPW), who had recently erected two Art Deco successes, the Civic Opera House and the Foreman State National Bank Building. Simpson, who was chairman of the Chicago Plan Commission from 1926 to 1935, was an enthusiastic advocate for urban planning and a devotee of Daniel Burham's masterpiece, the 1909 Plan of Chicago, though, as one historian has put it, Simpson's beliefs were "tempered by an intense, no-nonsense pragmatism."[3] It made sense he would choose Burnham's successor firm for the warehouse.

As with the Civic Opera House, the inventive Alfred Shaw of GAPW was put in charge of the design. The 61,000 steel elements were made by McClintic-Marshall, a firm specializing in bridge building, and erected by a crew of more than 2,500 workers. Partially assembled components were built off-site and hauled in by truck, rail, and barge.[4] The building came in at a cost of $38 million. It has a total floor space of four million square feet, which is about ninety-two acres (a football field is 1.32 acres). The building was the larg-

Opposite: One of the most elegant corporate showrooms in the Merchandise Mart was that of the glass company Libby-Owens-Ford. HB-04741-A, Chicago History Museum, Hedrich-Blessing Collection; Giovanni Suter, photographer.

The Merchandise Mart contained the world's biggest broadcasting studio, a concert hall large enough for symphony orchestras to air live concerts. Merchandise Mart, National Broadcasting Company Studio, Chicago, Illinois. Graham, Anderson, Probst, White, architects. Ryerson and Burnham Libraries Book Collection, Ryerson and Burnham Art and Architecture Archives, The Art Institute of Chicago. Digital File # 000000.090520_148.

est in the world in terms of floor space, although the Pentagon surpassed it in 1943. Like the Chicago Daily News Building, it made use of the air rights above a railroad—in this case the Chicago and North Western Railway. The building rests on supports twenty feet tall, leaving ample room for the trains underneath, trains that proved indispensable for hauling in construction materials at first and then merchandise.

Writing in *The Western Architect* in 1930, Superintendent Sengstock said,

> The Merchandise Mart is constructed of steel, concrete, and stone, with wrought iron trim at the entrances. It rests upon 458 reinforced caissons with truncated cone spreading bases, reaching 80 to 100 feet below street level. . . . The interior is intersected by spacious corridors, veritable business streets, extending for more than 650 feet on each floor. Bordering upon these great galleries are hundreds of wholesale stores, showing by day and by night, hundreds of lines of merchantable wares. It is estimated that six and one-half miles of windows will constantly display merchandise along

these magnificent inside thoroughfares. The corridors have impressive architectural treatment and brilliant illumination.[5]

Several commentators at the time said the Merchandise Mart was more than a building, it was a city; even better, it was a "planned community," one that used modern science and rationality to achieve the greatest efficiency. As large as Field's business was, it wasn't large enough to occupy the entire building—nor was it intended to. Management welcomed other wholesalers—1,500 of them, it was reported at the time—who set up shop on the Mart's interior "rainless streets," as the owners called them. It was "an age of increased efficiency through consolidation," as one Field executive explained, and according to architectural historian Jay Pridmore, "the idea was to make the Mart the wholesaling center of the world."[6]

In addition, it was a multiuse building, also containing office space, a department store, and on the nineteenth floor, broadcasting studios—first for radio stations and then television. The building contained the world's biggest broadcasting studio, a concert hall large enough for symphony orchestras to air live concerts. The Compound and Pyrono Door Co. of St.

The facade once displayed fifty-six representations of Native American chiefs, which were removed during a 1961 renovation. DN-0091412, Chicago Sun-Times/Chicago Daily News collection, Chicago History Museum.

Joseph, Michigan, supplied no fewer than fifty-seven soundproof doors for the space.

The facade of the building is somewhat stark, without the ingenious handling of forms that characterize the Daily News Building. Yet it has grandeur. It has four thousand windows, and it is eighteen stories high with an additional six stories in the central tower, which is capped with a pyramidal roof. On the twenty-second and twenty-fourth floors of the facade were once fifty-six large heads of Native American chiefs; these were unfortunately removed during a 1961 renovation, depriving the building of an eye-catching decorative scheme, although it was difficult to see from the street. According to Jean L. Guarino, the Merchandise Mart "exemplifies restrained Art Deco at its best, with smooth walls of gray limestone, vertical piers, shallow upper-floor setbacks, and spare use of non-historical detailing." As in several other Chicago Art Deco skyscrapers, the facade has a three-part scheme of a base, shaft, and capital. Decorating the surface are bands of chevrons and bronze diamonds.[7] The building's corners are embellished with four chamfered turrets—that is, the corners are cut off at 45-degree angles. Like the earlier Wrigley Building and Palmolive Building, the Mart was illuminated, and it still makes an exhilarating display at night when it's reflected in the river.

When the building was opened, the neighborhood to the north wasn't much. Going from east to west, you would find an artsy neighborhood known as Tower Town and then the "furnished room" district, mostly once-elegant, now shabby, homes subdivided into rooms to rent. North Clark Street contained cheap hotels where rooms could be had for twenty-five to seventy-five cents a night. Toward the north branch of the river was the slum, a.k.a. "Little Hell." Consequently, the rear of the Mart was purely functional. When the area became the chic River North neighborhood, building management installed enticing entrances to draw pedestrians from that side.

Still, the building is best entered from the riverfront so as to experience the splendid two-story lobby. It contains seventeen mural panels by Jules Guérin, who might have received the commission because he had done the bravura illustrations for the Plan of Chicago, which Simpson so admired. The lobby scenes depict commerce in the past and around the world: freighters on the Rhine, a camel caravan proceeding past an Egyptian pyramid, and so on. The elegantly colored, almost pastel, panels portray, according to Deborah Fulton Rau, "commerce throughout the world, including the countries whence came most of the goods sold in the building. The murals depict the principal industries and products, the primary mode of transportation, and the architecture of fourteen countries . . . they connect the modern world of the Mart with the distant and the past."[8] They were placed rather high, which has made them a bit hard to appreciate, and the original, inadequate lighting didn't help.

Although the great structure was successful in attracting tenants in its first year, its intended aim of becoming the mother of all warehouses was not achieved. The idea for the Mart, ironically, came about when Marshall Field & Co.'s wholesale business, which had once been much bigger than the company's retail business, was declining. Many stores in the midsize cities of the Midwest had discovered the advantages of buying directly from factories rather than from middlemen; mail-order houses like Chicago-based Sears, Roebuck and Co. cut into retail stores' profits.

And then the Great Depression gave Field's wholesale business the coup de grâce. The Field Company got out of wholesaling altogether in 1936, and the Merchandise Mart sat practically empty. It would not be until after World War II that it finally attained success. The Mart was purchased by Joseph Kennedy, the patriarch of the famous political family, and merchants and designers once again filled its halls, as they do today. Kennedy introduced the concept of using the Mart for trade shows, which drew manufacturers from across the nation. Furniture companies, espe-

Opposite: The Merchandise Mart has chamfered corners (cut on the diagonal), a classic Art Deco feature. Merchandise Mart, Chicago, Illinois. Graham, Anderson, Probst, White, architects. Historic Architecture and Landscape Image Collection, Ryerson and Burnham Art and Architecture Archives, The Art Institute of Chicago. Digital File # M525185.

The grand entryway of the Merchandise Mart as seen in the 1930s. Merchandise Mart, Chicago, Illinois. Graham, Anderson, Probst, White, architects. Ryerson and Burnham Libraries Book Collection, Ryerson and Burnham Art and Architecture Archives, The Art Institute of Chicago. Digital File # 000000.090520_141.

The lobby of the Merchandise Mart displays seventeen mural panels by Jules Guérin representing commerce around the world. This one depicts life in the Netherlands. Photograph by the author.

cially, found the building accommodating. The Mart turned out to be perfectly adaptable.

In the first decades of the twenty-first century, the building unexpectedly became "hip," as David Roeder of the *Chicago Sun-Times* put it.[9] Vornado Realty Trust, which had purchased the building from the Kennedys in 1998, put $40 million into a restoration project that included a wide staircase connecting to the lobby. Three restorers from the Conservation Center painstakingly swabbed the Guérin murals with cotton swabs; then a new coat of varnish was applied and better lighting installed. According to a *Chicago Tribune* reporter, "Chocolate Arabian skies have lightened. Once dimly etched pyramids now pop in mustard yellows."[10] Vornado then added another $40 million to give "The Mart" (as they rechristened it) the trendy amenities coveted by contemporary office staffs—retailers, two kinds of bars (alcohol and juice), a lounge with a river view, a pedestrian plaza and lawn, a conference center, a café, and "Art on the Mart," a system of nighttime digital projections with the building's massive facade as a screen. Innovative tenants responded and the building welcomed companies such as PayPal, Allstate, Grainger, and the nonprofit tech startup incubator 1871, which gave us the parking app SpotHero.

Several of Chicago's Art Deco skyscrapers are examples of adaptive reuse, but the Merchandise Mart still fulfills its original purpose as a showcase for design firms and similar enterprises. But it does so in a fresh way. So it's adaptive because it adapts—to changing times.

LOYOLA

No. 18

LAWSON HOUSE YMCA

PERKINS, CHATTEN & HAMMOND, 1931

When Chicago investors planned an Art Deco skyscraper, they wanted it to be in a good part of town. When officials of the YMCA planned *their* Chicago Art Deco skyscraper, they wanted it to be in a *bad* part of town. At that time, the northeast corner of Chicago Avenue and Dearborn Street fit the bill.

To live today in the stylish quarter around the Lawson House YMCA requires substantial means. The area is known as Near North, and it boasts Michelin-starred restaurants, posh condominiums, and groceries that sell imported pâté with truffles. But, just to show how cities can change, in the 1920s the area was anything but chic—it was pretty rough, in fact.

Why choose such a dicey area? As John V. Farwell, president of the board of trustees, explained, "We chose the site near the gangland district because we thought much could be done for the younger boy of the locality." W. J. Parker, general secretary of the YMCA, explained that the YMCA was "developing keener appreciation of the people of different races, nationalities, religions, and occupations"—a progressive attitude for 1930. Parker went on to explain that the growing YMCA membership in Chicago numbered

A limestone frieze of athletes above the third floor of the Lawson House. Photograph by Terence Faircloth, Atelier Teee, Inc.

just over thirty thousand, and one-third were boys under eighteen. A *Chicago Tribune* story was titled "Y.M.C.A. Plans to Oust Gangs with Athletics."[1] A similar headline could be written today.

Parker's sentiment was in keeping with the long tradition of the Young Men's Christian Association, which was founded in London in 1844 with the express purpose of offering young men a refuge from the rough city streets and providing spiritual guidance. The organization expanded to Chicago as early as 1858, and the first Chicago YMCA building, on Madison Street between La Salle and Clark, opened in 1867. By 1930, when the Lawson House building opened, the YMCA had seventeen centers in the Windy City and, despite the organization's name, offered classes for women and girls. The Lawson House YMCA reached out to two quite different groups. As a means to "oust gangs with athletics" it offered recreational facilities to slum kids, but as a residence it was meant to attract unmarried, white-collar male employees and students at Chicago's distinguished professional schools, such as the nearby Northwestern University Medical School.[2]

Outside the Lawson House, the most noteworthy Y in Chicago was the Wabash Avenue YMCA, which is now on the National Register of Historic Places. Funded by philanthropist and Sears executive Julius Rosenwald, it catered to African Americans arriving from the American South during the Great Migration of the 1920s. It not only offered shelter, recreation, and job training to Black newcomers but also helped them find employment—particularly in the meatpacking industry. It was at the Wabash Avenue YMCA in 1926 that Carter G. Woodson established "Negro History Week," which eventually became Black History Month.

The start of construction of the Lawson House building was funded by a bequest from Victor F. Lawson, publisher of the *Chicago Daily News* and a founder of the Associated Press, who died in August 1925 and who, according to John Farwell, was "the friend of young boys" (he also founded the Daily News Fresh Air Fund). According to Emmett Dedmon's history of the YMCA in Chicago, the value of this bequest was $3,590,571—the "largest single benefaction in the history of the YMCA of Metropolitan Chicago."[3]

Work began late in 1929. On February 8, 1930, as workers were installing the caissons to support the building, two horrific explosions occurred, burning four men. The most severely burned was Barney Gallagher, who was working at the bottom of the caisson and was knocked unconscious as flames shot 120 feet high. The blasts were heard across the north side and shattered windows in nearly two dozen neighboring buildings. It was thought that the explosions were the result of a short circuit in an electrical wire.[4]

The blasts were not the only difficulty presented by the laying of the foundation. According to a newspaper story, "For a long while it looked as if there wouldn't be any completion for the gigantic structure, as the pile drivers kept pushing the long poles down into the mucky earth. The pit that seemed bottomless, however, was finally filled, after 1,413 piles had been driven and a concrete mat poured."[5]

When the Lawson House YMCA was dedicated on November 1, 1931, it was the largest such facility in the world, with accommodations for 735 men. The structure was considered wonderfully "moderne" and comparable to a swanky private men's club. Each of the first eighteen floors of the building contained thirty-seven rooms, each about eleven by fifteen feet. The floors grew smaller at floor nineteen, and from nineteen to twenty-two the lodging floors contained eleven rooms. The 650 rooms were small but had first-rate amenities—for example, a radio speaker with five channels. Small, unobtrusive closets cleverly concealed hot and cold running water taps, and some rooms had showers. The building offered seven hundred telephones with outside lines, a thirteenth-floor roof garden, meeting rooms, a chapel for meditation, a library, two gymnasiums, a boxing ring, a rifle range, a large swimming pool with a deep diving area, handball and volleyball courts, restaurants and cafeterias, and ten studios for music, hobbies, and the like. Two curious features were a futuristic "room of 1950" described as "ultra-modernistic" and a "log cabin" room with timber on the walls and an artificial woodland view out the window. The log cabin room was one of a set of three historically themed spaces that also included a Tudor room with half-timbered walls and a Renaissance

A contemporary postcard displaying the features of the Lawson House YMCA when it was new. The 650 rooms were small but had first-rate amenities, such as a radio speaker and hot and cold running water. Some rooms even had showers. Author's collection.

Left: Art Deco fountain in the Lawson House YMCA. Photograph by the author.

Below: Art Deco rendering of an athlete in the Lawson House YMCA. Photograph by the author.

room. Victor Lawson's brother Ivor donated five thousand books to a Lawson Memorial Library.

The building is nearly a square (150 by 104 feet) and is a characteristically stepped-back Art Deco tower of twenty-four stories.[6] The architectural firm was Perkins, Chatten & Hammond, recent designers of the Northwest Tower. The skyscraper consists of a three-story limestone base below a tower of russet-colored brick with cast iron and terra-cotta trim. The symmetrical main facade on Chicago Avenue is ingeniously varied with alternating projecting piers and recessed spandrels. The entry door is modest, but above it are impressive panels decorated with chevron patterns and central panels with a large Y. Above the large third-floor windows are three characteristically Art Deco limestone sculptural reliefs, each depicting an athlete. Other Art Deco touches are the chevrons and fluted pilasters. The top of the setback tower has no windows but three vertical piers that culminate at the roof.

The Lawson House YMCA served Chicago well for decades, operating as a full-service hotel during the Great Depression, accommodating many visitors to the Century of Progress Exposition in 1933–1934, and transitioning to housing during and after World War II. With 583 apartments, it was the largest single-room occupancy (SRO) building in the city. By the twenty-first century, however, the YMCA was deaccessioning its SRO facilities. It vacated the Lawson House in 2013 and sold it to Peter Holsten of Holsten Human Capital Development, who had an admirable track record of providing "affordable, market rate, mixed-income and mixed-use housing," for the grand sum of one dollar.

Holsten's plan was to convert the SRO facilities into 409 "micro apartments" measuring three hundred square feet (more than double the size of the original housing units) with kitchenettes, toilets, private baths, a bed, a wardrobe, chairs, and a kitchen table. The YMCA had required Holsten to promise to offer affordable units for households at or below 60 percent of the Area Median Income. To finance the restoration and conversion, Holsten secured a $17.6 million loan from the city, a $17.2 million loan from the Illinois Housing Development Authority, and a $79.4 million loan from Chase Bank. The developer also received $12.4 million in historic preservation tax credits. According to Holsten Human Capital Development, the project received the largest single allocation of Low-Income Housing Tax Credits in the history of Illinois.

Holsten completed the relocation of the 382 existing residents in October 2021, and the work began, with the restorers using documentation from 1931. The facade was carefully restored and the windows were replaced. Three new stair towers were installed, the main entrance was moved from Chicago Avenue around the corner to the much quieter Dearborn Street, retail space and bicycle storage were installed on the ground floor, the Art Deco chapel was skillfully restored, and the rooftop terrace on the nineteenth floor setback was refurbished. A laundry room, fitness center, and residents' lounge were added on each floor. Especially welcome was the installation of in-unit air-conditioning. Lawson House reopened in 2024, with many of the previous tenants returning to much-improved facilities.

A small but efficient Lawson House apartment after the recent renovation. Courtesy of Jackie Taylor Holsten.

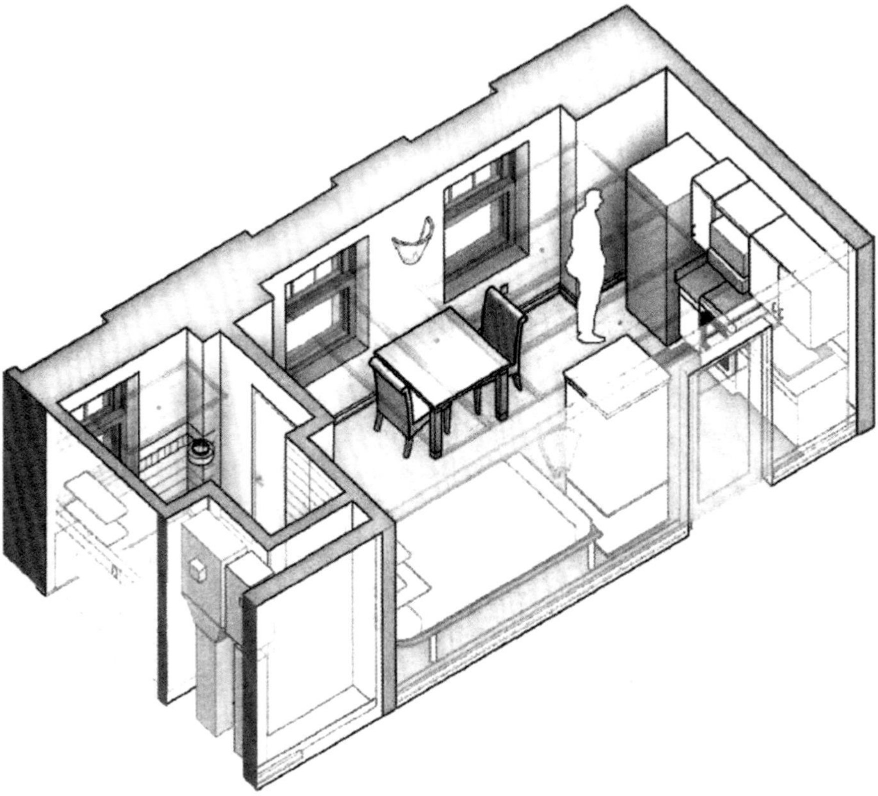

Nº. 19

CENTRAL POST OFFICE

GRAHAM, ANDERSON, PROBST & WHITE, 1934

Architect Daniel Burnham famously said, "Make no little plans," a quotation that has inspired generations of Chicagoans.

The US Congress tried to ignore the advice. When, in 1917, Congress appropriated $4.25 million for the construction of a new main post office in Chicago, city planners were determined not to go halfway but to put up a post office that would last. Appearing at a hearing before the US House of Representatives, Charles H. Wacker, chairman of the Chicago Plan Commission, echoed Burnham and warned, "You cannot build too big to meet future needs. . . . The story of Chicago's successive post office buildings is one chapter of inadequacy after another."[1]

Congress did greenlight the new post office, but it did so only as a facility for parcel post. Other mail would be handled as it always had been—at the downtown Federal Building, an attractive 1905 Beaux-Arts construction designed by Henry Ives Cobb. (It was replaced in 1965 by a Miesian-style complex, which most critics found disappointing.)

Sure enough, only a few years after its opening in 1921, the United States Mail Building, as it was called, was already inadequate. The city proposed an even bigger post office on the same site (on the west bank of the Chicago River between Van Buren and Harrison Streets). In effect, the 1921 post office was to be integrated into a newer one (a large six-story section of the old building can be seen today on the side facing the river). US Postmaster General Walter F. Brown laid the cornerstone on May 23, 1932.

Although New York City (6,930,446) had a much greater population than Chicago (3,376,438), Chicago's post office was the busiest in the country, handling 35 million letters and 500,000 sacks of packages *every day*. Much of this bulk came from the activities of Chicago's massive mail-order houses, including Montgomery Ward, Spiegel, and Sears, Roebuck and Co., which shipped out tons of catalogs and packages and received innumerable orders.

Like the recently constructed Chicago Daily News Building, the new post office was to be built over railroad tracks—a most practical arrangement because so much mail was shipped by rail. These were the tracks that ran into Union Station one block to the north, which had opened in 1925. It was estimated that using the railroad would eliminate at least five hundred daily truck trips through Chicago's clogged thoroughfares. As Postmaster General Brown explained, using trains would "eliminate the prodigal waste of time and money incident to the trucking of large amounts of bulk mail through the congested streets of our great cities."[2]

Fortunately, the structural engineer for the Chicago Union Terminal Company, which planned the new post office, was the same Joshua D'Esposito who had devised the ingenious system by which gas and smoke emissions from steam locomotives were vented up and out from the tracks below the Chicago Daily News Building. As D'Esposito explained the post office endeavor, "The project presents a maze of problems. One hundred caissons must be laid in a railroad over which there are between 300 and 400 train movements daily. From thirty to forty tons of steel must be erected over this yard without interruption of train movements. Then there is the problem of engine smoke, which must be drawn off by suction through vents in the ground floor of the building and carried in numerous small stacks to the roof."[3]

D'Esposito, born in Sorrento, Italy, in 1878, had one of those stirring immigrant success stories. He came to America at age nineteen. He learned English quickly and worked his way from Connecticut to Washington, DC, to Pittsburgh, steadily taking on more important building and designing jobs, and came to Chicago to be chief construction engineer for the new Union Station. He elected to remain in the Windy City, where he opened an office. Undoubtedly, his most popular project, for which he was the chief engineer, was the Sky Ride, the high-flying attraction of the Chicago Century of Progress Exposition of 1933–1934. It was a kind of aerial tramway, in which "rocket cars" traveled on cables suspended more than six hundred feet above the fairground lagoon.

The commission to design the new post office building went to Graham, Anderson, Probst & White, architects of the 1921 post office and designers of Union Station. Now fully operating in Art Deco mode, they conceived an edifice in the fashionable "moderne" style, as they had recently done for the Merchandise Mart.

Construction began in early 1931. The Great Depression was in full swing, so commendation of the new structure went not only to its efficiency and splendor, but also to the jobs it was creating—an estimated four to six thousand.[4] When the building was formally opened on September 28, 1934, it was the largest post office in the world, with fifty acres of floor space. More than 125 trains and 6,000 trucks entered and departed every day. The building contained ten miles of conveyor belts, forty-eight elevators, a café, and a branch of the Chicago Public Library.[5] The heating system used 25.5 miles of pipe and employed a novel technology—the pipes were welded instead of being connected in the traditional way by gaskets and flanges. One can only wonder who counted them, but it was reported the system used 71,849 welds.[6]

The post office was constructed with a unique passageway under and through the building. The designers intended it for a roadway, but the project was not carried out until the construction of the Congress Expressway (now the Eisenhower Expressway), which

was opened in sections between 1955 and 1960. It carries traffic from the western suburbs right under the building, across a bridge, and into downtown.

Planners initially envisioned a six-acre landing field on the roof, although the *Chicago Tribune* explained

A huge innovative system of tubes was installed to handle the enormous amount of mail processed in the new Central Post Office. US Post Office (433 W. Van Buren), Chicago, Illinois. Graham, Anderson, Probst, White, architects. Historic Architecture and Landscape Image Collection, Ryerson and Burnham Art and Architecture Archives, The Art Institute of Chicago. Digital File # 60323.

Above: The busy entry doors of Chicago's new Central Post Office in 1932. US Post Office (433 W. Van Buren), Chicago, Illinois. Graham, Anderson, Probst, White, architects. Ryerson and Burnham Libraries Book Collection, Ryerson and Burnham Art and Architecture Archives, The Art Institute of Chicago. Digital File # 000000.090520_100.

Opposite: The floor of the post office lobby bears an appropriate Art Deco compass symbolizing the vast reach of the postal service. Photograph by Andrea Blatz.

that "aviators generally do not believe the roof to be of sufficient area for landing." Still, it was reported, "numerous plane manufacturers are experimenting with devices intended to stop a plane soon after it comes down."[7] It sounds frightening. The aircraft that was needed was the helicopter, which was still a decade away. In 1938 an autogiro (a predecessor of the modern helicopter) landed on the building's roof. But this was a demonstration, not an ongoing service, and it was not until the 1940s and 1950s that whirlybirds regularly used the space. The first helicopter landing on the post office roof was on October 1, 1946; it had flown from New York City by way of Cleveland. Among those to greet the craft was none other than famed aviation pioneer Igor Sikorsky, who around 1940 had developed at his Connecticut factory the first practical helicopter. After leaving the post office, the helicopter then proceeded to fly to the roof of the Merchandise Mart, which was so large it had its own post office. Into the 1950s, helicopters were used to ship mail to nearby cities like Joliet and Waukegan.

ELEVATOR

This spread: The lobby of the Central Post Office displays Art Deco renderings of the various ways in which the mail was delivered. Photographs by Andrea Blatz.

The building's exterior, clad in gray Indiana limestone with a black granite base (the "Grand Art Deco formula"), is separated into three tiers: the base (with sixteen-foot-tall windows), the shaft, and the capital.[8] The main bulk is nine stories (190 feet) high, and twelve-story (230-foot) towers, originally used for offices, stand at each of the four corners. An expansive seven-step granite staircase leads up to the principal entrance, which is on Van Buren Street and has eleven bronze portals, although not all are entry doors. Dramatic lofty vertical window bands give a lift to the exceptionally wide facade. The exterior ornamentation is limited, but the interior is showy, with its varied types of marble and ceramic tiles. The 350-foot-long lobby, which has dramatic 38-foot-high ceilings and white marble walls of Alabama madre cream, runs the length of the building, which bestows a definite grandeur. The multicolored checkerboard floor, made of Tennessee champion pink marble and Tavernelle marble with a green marble border, sports large abstract compass motifs, and the large hanging bronze and glass pendant lights have a classic geometric Art Deco form.[9] The interior is bedecked with plaques depicting various aspects of the mail service (railroad, steamship, airplane), some set in gold-glass mosaic walls.

Modern technologies, such as the invention of zip codes and modern automation systems, eventually rendered the post office building outmoded. The cost of adapting it to the latest technology was deemed too high, and a new post office, built with these systems in mind, was constructed across Harrison Street and opened in 1996. The old central post office sat unoccupied and deteriorating while city officials wondered what to do with such a massive empty space. Developers came forth with proposals—a hotel, an apartment or office building, an auto mall—but nothing panned out. It was being referred to as a "white elephant."

And then Bill Davies, a British real estate developer with no real ties to Chicago, bought the structure in 2009 for $24.8 million. He came up with the most daring scheme yet. With a price tag of $3.5 billion (not a misprint), it would straddle the Chicago River and have not one, but five, skyscrapers, the biggest topping out at two thousand feet (the tallest building

in North America). It would offer a slew of galleries, restaurants, theaters, office space, residences, and retail stores; parking for twelve thousand cars (again, not a misprint); and a six-level pedestrian bridge that would block views of the river—an "urban mecca," as it was ardently described. Estimated construction time: twenty years. Blair Kamin, architecture critic of the *Chicago Tribune*, was practically in shock, calling it a "financial fantasy" that "is as mediocre as it is megalomaniacal."[10] The Chicago Plan Commission actually approved the proposal, but funding proved unattainable. Davies held on to the fading property for more than six years, until, on May 13, 2016, he sold it to 601W Companies, a real estate firm based in New York City. Davies's dream died—and so did he, the very next day.

In 2017 the building was given landmark status, which protected it from overenthusiastic rebuilding, modernization, or partial demolition. Under its new owners, the old post office experienced a renaissance—to the tune of nearly a billion dollars—orchestrated by the Gensler architectural firm. It was reported to be the largest redevelopment project in the United States. The historic lobby was restored to its original glory. Major businesses, such as Walgreens, Uber Technologies, PepsiCo, and Ferrara Candy Company leased space. A food hall—virtually a contemporary necessity—was installed, and commuting tenants were reminded that the building was just a three-minute walk from Union Station. The icing on the cake was a feature dubbed the "Meadow"—a three-and-a-half-acre "urban rooftop oasis." Once again, helicopters landed on the post office roof. In this instance, they were bringing stuff *in*—more than ten thousand helicopter lifts supplied some fifty thousand cubic feet of soil and forty thousand plants. The verdant new space featured a basketball court, a quarter-mile walking path, "seating pods for employee collaboration," and in savvy deference to contemporary penchants, pickleball courts.

Although the building was once an "incredible bulk . . . that no one knew what to do with," according to Chicago business reporter David Roeder, "today, the Old Post Office is the capital of commercial hipness in Chicago."[11]

Nº. 20

FIELD BUILDING

GRAHAM, ANDERSON, PROBST & WHITE, 1934

Adjectives that have been used to describe the Field Building include *dignified*, *soaring*, *giant*, *imposing*, *huge*, *mammoth*, and *sleek*. Among the nouns: *simplicity*, *clarity*, *monumentality*, *modernity*. In 1997, John Zukowsky, then-curator of architecture at the Art Institute of Chicago, said, "This is our Empire State Building, the modern definition of a skyscraper, taking a whole block [and] beautifully proportioned."[1]

It was, as the newspapers noted when it opened, the largest office building in Chicago. The Merchandise Mart contained, of course, many more square feet, but at the time it was considered a warehouse, not an office building. Another laudable attribute of the Field Building was not something much mentioned during the buoyant twenties: jobs. But by the thirties, when so many workingmen were pounding the streets or selling apples, the Field Building would provide employment for no fewer than 7,500 "active workers."[2]

The name on the building was that of department store tycoon Marshall Field. Field himself died in 1906; the skyscraper was the project of the Field estate. The architects were Graham, Anderson, Probst & White (GAPW) and the designer was Alfred Shaw. They had just completed the Merchandise Mart, a Field's project, and had earlier done the Field Museum and the Shedd Aquarium (John G. Shedd had been president of the Marshall Field company). Also, D. H. Burnham, the predecessor firm to GAPW, had designed Field's State Street store.

Putting up the money for such a gigantic real estate project at a time when the world economy was plunging into an abyss took some nerve, although Marshall Field III, now in charge, was personally hardly damaged: his portfolio was diverse and his great wealth was mostly in real estate and bonds.[3] Still, he was worried. Ernest Graham's private secretary, Charles F. Murphy, went to consult with Field, who had moved to New York City:

> Field said to me, "You know, things look so bad I think I'm going to stop that job." They were already underway with the foundation. . . . when I got back to Chicago I told E.R. Graham. Graham said, "Marshall Field told me that you urged him to stop." I said, "He turned it around. He's the one that wants to stop. He is getting cold feet." So Graham had Howard White call in all the subcontractors. The contracts were practically all let. He asked them how much they wanted to cancel their contracts. He learned it would cost more to cancel the contracts than to go ahead with the building, so they went ahead and they were glad they did.[4]

One of the six structures demolished to make way for the Field Building was the historic Home Insurance Building of 1885. Some historians believe the Home Insurance Building was the first skyscraper, although others, as discussed in chapter 14, give that honor to Chicago's 1889 Tacoma Building. When work began on the Field Building, the *Chicago Tribune* observed, "the old argument as to which was the first office building of steel construction . . . apparently is coming to life again."[5] This "old argument" was not trivial in Chicago, where skyscraper history was serious business—serious enough that before the demolition began, the Field estate appointed a ten-member committee of specialists (including Graham) to study the Home Insurance Building as it was being dismantled and report on whether the construction techniques gave it historical priority. It was thought their findings might decisively establish that the building's importance in architectural history was "enormous."

Their analysis was painstaking: during the three-week demolition period they visited every day, taking measurements and photographs and making drawings, while the wrecking company took special care to expose the metal framing. The committee submitted its report on November 24, 1931, and concluded, "we have no hesitation in stating that the Home Insurance Building was the first high building to utilize as the *basic* principle of its design the method known as skeleton construction. . . . We are also of the opinion that owing to its priority and its immediate success and renown the Home Insurance Building was in fact the primal influence in the acceptance of skeleton construction: the true father of the skyscraper."[6] Today a plaque in the lobby explicates and repeats the committee's verdict.

In 1929 the architecture journal *Pencil Points* committed a historical faux pas by writing that the Tacoma Building was the first skyscraper. The publication was immediately called on it by none other than D. Everett Waid, who had actually worked in the Home Insurance Building some four decades before as a draftsman for William Le Baron Jenney, who had designed the edifice. When the Tacoma was under construction, he said, he was "personally a witness." He assured the editors the Home Insurance Building was the first skyscraper.[7]

Nevertheless, it came down. The speed of construction of the Field Building was unprecedented. According to a contemporary report in the *Chicago Tribune*, "The twenty-four stories of steel were erected in 40 working days, or 320 hours, against the previous average of seventy-five days for a similar project. The stone was laid at the rate of one floor a day, the fastest job ever done in Chicago."[8]

The skyscraper consists of a forty-three-story central tower with twenty-two-story modules at each corner. Skyscraper historian Joseph J. Korom Jr. has called it "five boxes glued together forming one super-sized skyscraper."[9] This configuration allowed for an uncommon number of corner offices—twelve

When the Home Insurance Building was demolished to make way for the Field Building, the owners appointed a committee to study the Home Insurance Building and report on whether the construction techniques made it history's first skyscraper. They did. Author's collection.

per floor.[10] As with most other Art Deco skyscrapers in Chicago, the tower is made of Indiana limestone and the base of black granite. The recessed window tiers and spandrels, alternating with the smooth limestone facade, create strong vertical upward movement. The imposing black frames of the two five-story entryways consist of a type of igneous rock then quarried in Wisconsin called Rosetta Black, which was cherished during the Art Deco era for its ability to acquire a high-gloss finish.[11]

Before the building was completed, a couple of images of it, including a postcard, were released; they don't include the grand entry doors, which indicates they were features added later in the design process. (It also indicates postcards might not always have the most reliable images.) The window and door frames on the ground floor are trimmed in white bronze. The 27-foot-high, 305-foot-long, bilevel lobby corridor, which runs the length of the building from La Salle Street to Clark Street, features floors of white marble terrazzo, panels of Paitone Breccia marble from Italy, and Colorado Yule Marble piers theatrically illuminated by floodlights. Mirrored pedestrian bridges sporting Art Deco clocks and nautical-style railings traverse the upper level. The escalators that go to the second floor were originally marble staircases. As Korom puts it, "Doorways, windows, mail boxes, signage, and elevator doors, all trimmed with brass and nickel, ooze Art Deco motifs."[12]

As might be expected for a skyscraper constructed so late in the Art Deco period, the building had advanced features, such as the use of aluminum, a cutting-edge material that had become affordable through new technology. As the *Architectural Record* explained in 1934, "Window frames for offices throughout are of aluminum, an innovation that contributes to ease of operation and improved lighting. Aluminum frames, because of their moderate sash width, permit a glass area 10 per cent greater than obtainable with wood frames. By precision in their manufacture there is virtually no rattle or air and dust leakage."[13] And because Chicago engineers were at the forefront of air-conditioning technology (as discussed in chapter 14), it's no surprise that the first four floors and basement of the Field Building were so equipped (the remainder followed in the 1960s).

BANK
1614
DISPATCH
773-685-2900

Opposite: The impressive black frames of the two five-story entryways, which were added late in the design process, are made from an igneous rock from Wisconsin called Rosetta Black. Library of Congress, Prints & Photographs Division, photograph by Carol M. Highsmith, LC-DIG-highsm-63022.

Above: Mirrored pedestrian bridges sporting Art Deco clocks and nautical-style railings traverse the upper level of the luminous twenty-seven-foot-high lobby that runs the length of the Field Building. Photograph by the author.

Much was made at the time of the forty-two specially ventilated elevators, which achieved a speed of one thousand feet per minute. One of the most felicitous touches came with the combination elevator indicator/post office box in the lobby, which is in the shape of the building itself. The large light panel marked the first time a visitor in a lobby could see what floor each elevator was on. The Field Building was the first in the Loop to use alternating electrical current, which, as the *Chicago Tribune* explained, "will enable tenants to enjoy the advantages of electric clocks, radios, and other electrical devices."[14] Finally, although new office buildings of today strive to provide tenants with all sorts of amenities, the Field Building was way ahead of them. Tenants had use of several restaurants, a barber shop, a beauty parlor, a telegraph office, a laundry, a florist, cigar and newsstands, squash and handball courts, and a gymnasium (men only, however).

Although the Field Company had offices in the building, it built the tower as a speculative real estate venture, not as corporate headquarters. And in the Great Depression that was a nail-biting proposition, especially because Field's, in an unusually

The Field Building contains what is probably the finest Art Deco mailbox in Chicago. The box is in the shape of the building itself. Photograph by Andrea Blatz.

self-sacrificing gesture, announced it would not accept occupants from other buildings. Also, despite his qualms, Marshall Field III did not try to build on the cheap. It was first-class all the way, and it made such an impression that it filled up with prestige tenants. One of the first was the well-known Attic Club, founded in 1923 and first headquartered on West Adams Street. It moved into the two penthouse floors and the new quarters were designed in a streamline style by architect David Adler. It became a gathering place for La Salle Street honchos, and it was said that "more business is done by brokers there than any other spot."[15]

The opening of the doors of the Field Building marked the close of an era. The skyscraper was the last of its kind—a farewell and bittersweet salute to an era of hope and splendor. Even before the first tenants moved in, it was already the final mile marker on a grand Art Deco highway that had begun just six years and one mile away.

CONCLUSION

The Field Building might have been Chicago's last Art Deco skyscraper, but the Art Deco spirit was hardly dead in the Windy City. It had a glorious swan song in the 1933–1934 Century of Progress Exposition, which stretched along the Lake Michigan shore from the Adler Planetarium south to 39th Street. The Art Deco buildings of this World's Fair were painted in bright colors, giving the event the nickname "Rainbow City," and miles of gas-filled tubes provided colored lighting.

Some of the architects who built Chicago's Art Deco skyscrapers contributed to the fair. The team of Edward H. Bennett, Hubert Burnham, and John Holabird, for example, designed both the Administration Building and the daring Travel and Transport Building, with its famous suspended dome. Holabird & Root designed the Chrysler Motors Building and the Gulf Oil Exhibit. The Burnham Brothers were responsible for the Firestone Building and the Sinclair Refining Company Building, and Andrew Rebori designed the naughty "Streets of Paris" show starring the famous fan dancer Sally Rand. Graham, Anderson, Probst & White were a little late to the party and

The Art Deco era in Chicago ended with the glorious display of the Century of Progress Exposition of 1933–1934, nicknamed the "Rainbow City." From the Newberry Library.

designed the Armour Building, which didn't open until the second year of the expo.[1]

Meanwhile, right up until World War II, Chicago factories continued to produce all sorts of household objects in the Art Deco style, many of which were fashioned from novel materials like aluminum, chrome, and Bakelite, which were ideal for the "streamline/moderne" look. Also, governments still had post offices, schools, and other structures to build, and many of these were in the Art Deco style or used Art Deco motifs. Chicago's Roseland Station Post Office, for example, built in 1936 and designed by John C. Bollenbacher, is a gem. Other later Chicago Art Deco structures include the 1937 terra-cotta Commercial Building on North Sheridan Road (Charles Andre Kristen) and the Fisher Studio Houses of the same year, the joint effort of Andrew Rebori and Edgar Miller.

But as for tall buildings, it would be more than two decades before another skyscraper, the Prudential Building, was built in the Windy City. By then, however, the architectural fashion was the International Style, a stripped-down aesthetic most identified with Mies van der Rohe, the German-born modernist architect who set up shop in Chicago in 1937 and inspired decades of steel-framed "glass boxes."

Even if the Great Depression hadn't suppressed funding for new buildings, the Art Deco style might well have died out anyway. In 1933, Henry-Russell Hitchcock and Philip Johnson mounted an exhibition at the Museum of Modern Art in New York titled "Early Modern Architecture: Chicago 1870–1910" that explicitly linked Mies's International Style to the so-called Chicago School of the late nineteenth century, which they saw as a forerunner of Miesian modernism. They made the case that the International Style, because it had American roots, was not some intrusive foreign import. Architect Jack Hartray is one of many who have criticized this once persuasive and widespread thesis as a "pure academic invention." "The commercial expansion of Chicago at the turn of the century had nothing to do with the social agenda of the Weimar Republic," he wrote, "and there is no reason to believe that Sullivan would have acknowledged [Walter] Gropius as his legitimate heir."[2]

Nevertheless, Art Deco became passé, a dangerous situation for buildings because they begin to look

Above and following page: Some Chicago Art Deco architects created pavilions for the Century of Progress. Holabird & Root designed the Chrysler Motors Building; the Burnham brothers did the Firestone Building; and the team of Edward H. Bennett, Hubert Burnham, and John Holabird were responsible for the Travel and Transport Building, with its innovative suspended dome. From the Newberry Library.

like candidates for demolition. But that didn't happen. According to cultural historian Neil Harris, "Fortunately, major deco buildings downtown were, for the most part, too recent, large, and well rented to be endangered."[3] So although a depressing number of the towers constructed during the first stage of skyscraper building in Chicago (c. 1885–1899) have been demolished, the Art Deco skyscrapers managed to ride out the wave of destruction that engulfed some historic Chicago buildings after World War II. This means they can be visited. The lobbies of the office buildings are mostly open, although those that are condo buildings are quite protective, and a visitor is unlikely to get as far as the elevators. At the time of this writing, three of the Art Deco skyscrapers—the Chicago Motor Club, the Carbide and Carbon Building, and the Northwest Tower—have found new life as hotels, which means one can even sleep in them, which was not the case when they were built. Meanwhile, the popularity of Art Deco has given rise to popular tours. All but three of the skyscrapers discussed in this book are in a compact area of downtown. The Chicago Art Deco Society has created two easy walking tours that include nearly all of them, and guided tours are available from the Chicago Architecture Center and other organizations.

Opposite: Chicago architects also kept Art Deco alive in more modest buildings, such as this bookstore by Holabird & Root. HB-03235-A, Chicago History Museum, Hedrich-Blessing Collection.

EVERY DAY CARDS
THE COMPLETE GARDEN
NOW
A Child's DICTIONARY
EVERY DAY CARDS
BARGAINS IN FINE BOOKS
3 GREAT BOOKS for YOUNG & OLD
AN ANTHOLOGY OF WORLD POETRY
BOULEVARD BOOKS
EVERY DAY CARDS
BIRDS OF AMERICA
Birds of America
MONOPOLY
A GUIDE TO CIVILIZED LEISURE
The EXILE

SKYSCRAPER BALLADE

Slim in her dress of carven stone,
Towering in the sky blue air,
Proud as a queen on her lofty throne,
Was ever a lady so tall and fair?
Well may the pygmy beneath her stare
As her ivory crown the white clouds kiss:
Still as a dream she rises there—
Where is the goddess divine as this?

As beauty should, she stands alone,
Unconcerned with any care;
She will be here when we are gone—
Was ever a lady so tall and fair?
She will remain when none knows where
The architect who dreamed her is . . .
Lights by night in her jeweled hair,
Where is the goddess divine as this?

When worms are gnawing the crumbling bone
Of architect and the millionaire
Who boasts this dream is his to own,
(Was ever a lady so tall and fair?)
Still the sunshine she shall share
When her builders the sun and starlight miss:
Rubies and mighty pearls she'll wear—
Where is the goddess divine as this?

RICHARD "RIQUARIUS" ATWATER,
THE CHICAGOAN, MAY 24, 1930

ACKNOWLEDGMENTS

This book wouldn't have been written without my longtime friend, the eminent intellectual historian James Sloan Allen. Although I was captivated by Art Deco in general and Chicago's skyscrapers in particular, I was reluctant to take on this project because I wasn't a professor of architectural history. "That's just why you *should* write it," Jim replied. I am also honored to call that celebrated historian of Chicago, Dominic Pacyga, a friend. It was he who urged me to send the idea for this book to the University of Chicago Press. He also introduced me to the Sky Ride Tap. At the University of Chicago Press, the proposal was championed by my outstanding editor, Timothy Mennel, who provided advice, corrections, suggestions, rewriting, information—well, the list goes on. Thanks also to Tim's worthy assistant, Andrea Blatz, who was always prompt in answering my sometimes pesky queries and guided me through technical details, and to my vigilant copyeditor, Lindsy Rice. Photographer Ian McClellan's stunning photographs speak for themselves. My gratitude also goes to those who invited me to visit and photograph some Art Deco skyscrapers—Jackie Taylor Holsten (Lawson House), Paula Duffy (Powhatan), Celia Marerro (Northwest Tower/Robey Hotel), and James "Red" Schmitt (Merchandise Mart). I also thank Dave Hofer of the Research Center of the Art Institute of Chicago, the rights and reproduction staff at the Chicago History Museum, and Emily Reiher, director of the Women and Leadership Archives at Loyola University (Mundelein Center), who was patient with my drawn-out queries. A big thanks to Joseph Loundy, president of the Chicago Art Deco Society; our meeting at the Art Deco Chicago Motor Club was a major incentive. It was a wonderful surprise when Barry Blackburn sent me a delightful cartoon of the activities of the traders at the Board of Trade. Mary and Michael Beyer provided encouragement and support, as did grandchildren Charles and Cecilia. And then there is my wife, Cathy. This book wouldn't exist without her—and I might not, either. She provided not only encouragement but also literary and technical assistance—taking photos, researching photographers, writing captions, messaging, and chauffeuring me around the Windy City. Love and appreciation to her.

NOTES

INTRODUCTION

1. Carla Breeze, *American Art Deco: Architecture and Regionalism* (W. W. Norton, 2003), 9.
2. "Skyscrapers," *Greater Chicago Magazine*, November 1929, 2.
3. Russell F. Whitehead, "Holabird and Root Masters of Design," *Pencil Points* 19, no. 2 (1938): 70.
4. Le Corbusier, *The Decorative Art of Today*, trans. James I. Dunnett (MIT Press, 1987), xxiii.
5. Quoted in John Zukowsky, David Van Zanten, and Carol Herselle Krinsky, *Chicago and New York: Architectural Interactions* (Art Institute of Chicago, 1984), 58.
6. Bevis Hillier, *Art Deco of the 20s and 30s* (Schocken Books, 1985), 11–12, 158.
7. Marvin D. Schwartz, "Antiques: Art Deco Show," *New York Times*, August 28, 1971, 22. The early 1970s, with the Vietnam War, political division, and widespread protests, was a stressful time; Schwartz was apparently hopeful that the optimistic spirit of Art Deco might offer a more positive impulse.
8. Evelyn Livingstone, "Art Imitates Fashion—and Vice Versa," *Chicago Tribune*, February 2, 1969, E1.
9. Bridget Elliott and Michael Windover, "What's the Use of Style? The Case of Art Deco," in *The Routledge Companion to Art Deco*, ed. Bridget Elliott and Michael Windover (Routledge, 2019), 1–10.
10. For descriptions of Art Deco in various world locations, including Latin America, East Asia, India, Australia, and South Africa, see Charlotte Benton, Tim Benton, and Ghislaine Wood, eds., *Art Deco 1910–1930* (V&A Publishing, 2015).
11. Jonathan M. Woodham, "From Pattern to Abstraction," in Benton, Benton, and Wood, *Art Deco 1910–1930*, 113.
12. W. Francklyn Paris, "Modernism," *Pencil Points* 11, no. 12 (1930): 954.
13. William L. Withuhn, *American Steam Locomotives: Design and Development, 1880–1960* (Indiana University Press, 2019), 345–47.
14. Bevis Hillier, *The World of Art Deco* (E. P. Dutton, 1971), 23.
15. François Mathey, *Les Années "25": Art Déco/Bauhaus/Stijl/Esprit Nouveau* (Musée des Arts Décoratifs, 1966), 9–10.
16. Alistair Duncan, *American Art Deco* (Harry N. Abrams, 1986), 22; "1,000 Viennese Artists Show Their Work; Beautiful Plastic Arts of the Wiener Werkstaette Exhibited by Joseph Urban," *New York Times*, June 14, 1922, 16.

17. Eleanor Jewett, "Art and Artists: Viennese Crafts in Rare Setting at Institute," *Chicago Tribune*, September 24, 1922, E20.
18. See Laura McGuire, "European Immigrant Designers and North American Art Deco," in Elliott and Windover, *Routledge Companion to Art Deco*.
19. McGuire, "European Immigrant Designers and North American Art Deco," 76.
20. "Oral History of John Augur Holabird," interview by Susan S. Benjamin, Chicago Architects Oral History Project, The Ernest R. Graham Study Center for Architectural Drawings, Department of Architecture, Art Institute of Chicago, 1993, 30.
21. Merve Buldaç, "Art Deco-Streamline Moderne Combination in Design: Analysis of the Floating Space SS Normandie From the Outside to the Inside," *Journal of Architectural Sciences and Applications* 9, no. 2 (2024): 1078–94.
22. See Pauline Saliga, "'To Build a Better Mousetrap': Design in Chicago, 1920–1970," in *Chicago Architecture and Design, 1923–1993: Reconfiguration of an American Metropolis*, ed. John Zukowsky (Prestel, 1993), 265–81.
23. Oriana Baddeley, "Ancient Mexican Sources of Art Deco," in Benton, Benton, and Wood, *Art Deco 1910–1930*, 58.
24. Lucy Fischer, "Art Deco and Cinema," in Elliott and Windover, *Routledge Companion to Art Deco*, 356.
25. Paul Kruty, "Midway Gardens," in *Art Deco Chicago*, ed. Robert Bruegmann (Chicago Art Deco Society, 2018), 80–83.
26. Quoted in Zukowsky, Van Zanten, and Krinsky, *Chicago and New York*, 84.
27. "A Skyscraper Survey," *American Builder*, August 1929, 59.
28. Carol Willis, "Light, Height, and Site: The Skyscraper in Chicago," in Zukowsky, *Chicago Architecture and Design*, 119.
29. "Construction Statistics," *Architectural Record*, August 1929, 152; "Wage Scales in the Building Trades," *Architectural Record*, March 1933, 28.
30. Thomas Leslie, *Chicago Skyscrapers 1871–1934* (University of Illinois Press, 2013), 151.
31. Charles G. Loring, "Office Buildings Now and Then," *Architectural Forum*, June 1930, 824.
32. Thomas E. Tallmadge, "The Development of the Office Building Since 1924," *Architectural Forum*, June 1930, 780.
33. Duncan, *American Art Deco*, 147.
34. Talbot F. Hamlin, "A Contemporary American Style," *Pencil Points* 19, no. 2 (1938): 70.
35. Mike Hope, *Art Deco Architecture: The Interwar Period* (Crowood Press, 2019), 57.
36. John Taylor Boyd, "Exhibition of the Chicago Architectural League," *Architectural Record*, August 1928, 161–62.
37. Edward Alden Jewell, "A Torch to Light Us," *New York Times*, December 1, 1929.
38. Lawrence Martin, "Chicago's Unlively Arts: A Sober Consideration of the Somewhat Civic Scene," *Chicagoan*, August 2, 1930, 9–10.
39. "A Distinctive American Architecture," *Architectural Forum*, August 1929, pt. 1, p. 35.
40. Leslie, *Chicago Skyscrapers*, 145.
41. W. A. Starrett, *Skyscrapers and the Men Who Build Them* (Barakaldo Books, 2002), 36.
42. Robert E. Schock and Eric J. Risberg, "120 Years of Caisson Foundations in Chicago," paper presented at the International Conference on Case Histories in Geotechnical Engineering, 2013, 6.
43. Frank A. Randall, *History of the Development of Building Construction in Chicago*, 2nd ed. (University of Illinois Press, 1999), 24; Robert D. Holtz, "Caissons in Chicago," *Ground Engineering*, January 1975, 19–23.
44. Paul Starrett, *Changing the Skyline: An Autobiography* (Whittlesey House, 1938), 172.
45. Starrett, *Skyscrapers and the Men Who Build Them*, 127.
46. Quoted in Roger Shepherd, ed., *Skyscraper: The Search for an American Style, 1891–1941* (McGraw-Hill, 2003), 258–59.

47. Raymond Wiggers, *Chicago in Stone and Clay: A Guide to the Windy City's Architectural Geology* (Northern Illinois University Press, 2022), 41.
48. Starrett, *Skyscrapers and the Men Who Build Them*, 228, 237.
49. Wiggers, *Chicago in Stone and Clay*, 142.
50. "Oral History of John Augur Holabird," 18.
51. Harry F. Cunningham, "Goodhue, the First True Modern," *Journal of the American Institute of Architects* 16, no. 7 (1928): 246.
52. Aliki Economides, "The Cormier Residence in Relief," in Elliott and Windover, *Routledge Companion to Art Deco*, 39.
53. Hildreth Meiere, "The Question of Decoration," *Architectural Forum*, July 1932, 1.
54. Duncan, *American Art Deco*, 148.
55. Rayne Adams, "Thoughts on Modern, and Other, Ornament," *Pencil Points* 10, no. 1 (1920): 16.
56. Aficionados of Art Deco will be interested to know that GAPW were the architects of the Shedd Aquarium (1929).
57. John Wellborn Root, "John Augur Holabird—An Appreciation," *Journal of the American Institute of Architects* 4, no. 5 (1945): 217.
58. "Oral History of T. Clifford Noonan," Chicago Architects Oral History Project, The Ernest R. Graham Study Center for Architectural Drawings, Department of Architecture, Art Institute of Chicago, 1995, 3.
59. "Oral History of John Augur Holabird," 67.
60. Randall, *History of the Development of Building Construction in Chicago*, 467.
61. Patricia Bayer, *Art Deco Architecture: Design, Decoration and Detail from the Twenties and Thirties* (Harry N. Abrams, 1992), 12.
62. Hope, *Art Deco Architecture*, 25.
63. Jay Pridmore and George A. Larson, *Chicago Architecture and Design* (Abrams, 2018), 129.
64. Pridmore and Larson, *Chicago Architecture and Design*, 72.
65. Whitehead, "Holabird and Root Masters of Design," 68.
66. "Oral History of Charles F. Murphy," Chicago Architects Oral History Project, The Ernest R. Graham Study Center for Architectural Drawings, Department of Architecture, Art Institute of Chicago, 1995, 34.
67. Editorial, *Chicagoan*, June 6, 1929, 7.
68. "Planners Make Chicago a City of True Dreams," *Chicago Tribune*, January 10, 1932, 9.
69. "Sees Chicago Nearer World Supremacy Goal," *Chicago Tribune*, January 1, 1930, 20.

ONE

1. "333 North Michigan Avenue, Chicago," *Architectural Record*, February 1929, 157.
2. Kheir Al-Kodmany, *Tall Buildings and the City: Improving the Understanding of Placemaking, Imageability, and Tourism* (Springer, 2020), 151.
3. "The Holabird & Root Exhibition, November 21–December 12," *Architectural Forum*, December 1929, pt. 1, p. 33.
4. Editorial, *Chicagoan*, March 1, 1930, 4.
5. Pauline A. Saliga, ed., *The Sky's the Limit: A Century of Chicago Skyscrapers* (Rizzoli, 1990), 296.
6. Ernest Fuller, "Famous Chicago Buildings," *Chicago Tribune*, May 23, 1959, A5; John W. Stamper, *Chicago's North Michigan Avenue: Planning and Development, 1900–1930* (University of Chicago Press, 1991), 151.
7. Raymond Wiggers, *Chicago in Stone and Clay: A Guide to the Windy City's Architectural Geology* (Northern Illinois University Press, 2022), 42.
8. "333 North Michigan Avenue, Chicago," 157.

9. Gladys E. Hamlin, *The Sculpture of Fred and Mabel Torrey* (Borden, 1969), xii. Torrey became something of a specialist in statues of Abraham Lincoln.
10. Different sources given different titles for the panels. I use the ones from Hamlin.
11. "Fred M. Torrey's Decorative Panels for a Chicago Sky-Scraper," *American Magazine of Art*, September 1928, 483–88.
12. Charles Collins, "Floreat Taberna," *Chicagoan*, September 22, 1928, 12.
13. They suffered from the weather over the years and were put in storage, but they were restored and returned to their original site in 2024. A large statue of a ram cracked during reinstallation but was found to be reparable. Lee Bey, "A Crack Spoils an 85-year-old Edgar Miller Sculpture's Homecoming. For Now, At Least," *Chicago Sun-Times*, December 23, 2024, 16–17.
14. Marin R. Sullivan, "Edgar Miller: Anti-Modern," *Chicago Art Deco Society Magazine*, Fall/Winter 2024, 16–19.
15. Eleanor Jewett, "Tavern Murals of Love Really Pageant of Life," *Chicago Tribune*, June 18, 1935, 13.
16. Jim L. Zimmer, "John Warner Norton: A Lockport Legacy," *Living Museum* 53, no. 4 (1991): 51–54. As far as art historians have been able to determine, Norton completed twenty-seven mural commissions.
17. Alan G. Artner, "Norton Rediscovery Lives Up to its Advance Billing," *Chicago Tribune*, August 21, 1992, F55.
18. Jim L. Zimmer, *John Warner Norton* (Illinois State Museum, 1993), 44.
19. Although the Tavern Club still operates, both the Norton and Miller murals are gone.

TWO

1. H. M. Brown, "Chicago Motor Club Opens New Downtown Home," *Chicago Tribune*, January 27, 1929, G14.
2. Patricia Bayer, *Art Deco Architecture: Design, Decoration and Detail from the Twenties and Thirties* (Harry N. Abrams, 1992), 167–68.
3. Jim L. Zimmer, *John Warner Norton* (Illinois State Museum, 1993), 24.
4. Paul Alessandro, "The Rebirth of the Chicago Motor Club," *Chicago Art Deco Society Magazine*, Fall 2015, 25–27.
5. Blair Kamin, "Chicago Motor Club Building, an Art Deco Gem, Revived as Hotel," *Chicago Tribune*, May 19, 2015, 14.

THREE

1. Philip Hampson, "City to Have Gay Colored Skyscraper," *Chicago Tribune*, February 12, 1928, B1.
2. Charles E. White Jr., "Architectural Terra Cotta," in *Common Brick Work Architectural Terra Cotta*, ed. William S. Lowndes (International Textbook, 1920), 2.
3. W. A. Starrett, *Skyscrapers and the Men Who Build Them* (Barakaldo Books, 2002), 125.
4. Jean L. Guarino, "Carbide and Carbon Building," in *Art Deco Chicago*, ed. Robert Bruegmann (Chicago Art Deco Society, 2018), 149.
5. Philip Berger, "Terra Infirma," *Chicago Tribune*, October 27, 2002, SM18.
6. Phat X. Chiem, "Terra-cotta Fragment Falls From Building, Hurts Woman," *Chicago Tribune*, February 1, 1999, C3.
7. Al Chase, "Twenty Story Flat Building for State-Elm," *Chicago Tribune*, August 30, 1927, 22.
8. John Zukowsky, "The Capitals of American Architecture: Chicago and New York," in

Chicago and New York: Architectural Interactions by John Zukowsky, David Van Zanten, and Carol Herselle Krinsky (Art Institute of Chicago, 1984), 20.

9. Laurie McGovern Petersen, ed., *AIA Guide to Chicago*, 4th ed. (University of Illinois Press, 2022), 165.
10. Hampson, "City to Have Gay Colored Skyscraper," B1.
11. Neil Harris, *Chicago Apartments: A Century and Beyond of Lakefront Luxury* (University of Chicago Press, 2020), 7.
12. Harris, *Chicago Apartments*, 7.

FOUR

1. "The Skyscraper Leaves the Loop," *Greater Chicago Magazine*, February 1929, 7.
2. Dominic A. Pacyga, *American Warsaw: The Rise, Fall, and Rebirth of Polish Chicago* (University of Chicago Press, 2019), 47–112.
3. "Wicker Park Facts," *Greater Chicago Magazine*, February 1929, 5.
4. "West Side Show Big Realty Gains," *Chicago Tribune*, June 30, 1912, G3.
5. "Joseph R. Noel Sees a Bright Future for Wicker Park," *Greater Chicago Magazine*, February 1929, 15.
6. "The Skyscraper Leaves the Loop," 9.
7. Al Chase, "Trio of Imposing Buildings for Neighborhood Centers," *Chicago Tribune*, May 20, 1928, B1.
8. "The Skyscraper Leaves the Loop," 7.

FIVE

1. Electus D. Litchfield, "Cooperative Apartments," *Architectural Forum*, September 1930, 313.
2. Harvey Warren Zorbaugh, *The Gold Coast and the Slum: A Sociological Study of Chicago's Near North Side* (University of Chicago Press, 1929; repr., 1976), 7.
3. Carroll William Westfall, "Apartments," in *The Encyclopedia of Chicago*, ed. James R. Grossman, Ann Durkin Keating, and Janice L. Reiff (University of Chicago Press, 2004), 26.
4. Ruth G. Bergman, "Home Suite Home II: Co-Operating in the Co-Op," *Chicagoan*, September 24, 1927, 19.
5. Carl W. Condit, *Chicago, 1910–29: Building, Planning, and Urban Technology* (University of Chicago Press, 1973), 304.
6. Henry Wright, "The Place of the Apartment in the Modern Community," *Architectural Record*, March 1930, 207.
7. Neil Harris, *Chicago Apartments: A Century and Beyond of Lakefront Luxury* (University of Chicago Press, 2020), 6.
8. Quoted in Harris, *Chicago Apartments*, 6.
9. "20,000 People Live in Chicago's 100% Co-ops, Survey Says," *Chicago Tribune*, July 27, 1930, A12.
10. Harry A. Rick, "Is There a 'Joker' in the Co-op Apartment Proposition?," *Chicago Tribune*, July 31, 1927, 16.
11. Ruth G. Bergman, "Home Suite Home: Building for the (Family) Ages," *Chicagoan*, July 30, 1927, 32.
12. Ruth G. Bergman, "Home Suite Home III: The Little Matter of Money," *Chicagoan*, October 8, 1927, 15.
13. "Criticism of Apartment Architecture," *Architectural Forum*, September 1930, 271–72.

14. Bergman, "Home Suite Home III," 29.
15. Timothy Barton, "Powhatan Apartments," Preliminary Staff Summary of Information Submitted to the Commission on Chicago Landmarks, November 1991.
16. Philip Hampson, "American Architecture and Design Features of New Co-op," *Chicago Tribune*, September 25, 1927, B1.
17. Teri J. Edelstein, "The Powhatan," in *Art Deco Chicago*, ed. Robert Bruegmann (Chicago Art Deco Society, 2018), 138.
18. Mary Lackritz Gray, *A Guide to Chicago's Murals* (University of Chicago Press, 2001), 172.
19. Neil Harris, *Chicago Apartments: A Century of Lakefront Luxury* (Acanthus Press, 2004), 66.
20. Sally A. Kitt Chappell, "Robert De Golyer's Light-Filled, Lakefront Classic," 3750 Lake Shore Drive, Inc., August 3, 2017, https://www.3750lsd.net/3750-north-lake-shore-drive-robert-de-golyers-light-filled-lakefront-classic/.

SIX

1. "Green 'nd Gold Tower Newest for Boul Mich," *Chicago Tribune*, May 13, 1928, B1. "Boul Mich," nickname of the Boulevard Saint-Michel in Paris, was a popular designation for Michigan Avenue before World War II.
2. The diaries and other papers of Daniel Burnham Jr. and Hubert Burnham are in the Ryerson and Burnham Art and Architecture Archives of the Art Institute of Chicago. A summary of Daniel Burnham Jr.'s diaries may be viewed online on the institute's website at https://www.artic.edu/artworks/262167/daniel-h-burnham-jr-and-hubert-burnham-papers.
3. Joseph J. Korom Jr., *The American Skyscraper, 1850–1940: A Celebration of Height* (Branden Books, 2008), 388.
4. Blair Kamin, "Rock Deco: Carbide and Carbon Building Keeps the Fizz as It's Remixed into the Hard Rock Hotel," *Chicago Tribune*, January 18, 2004, E1.

SEVEN

1. Although the name of the company that built the building was Colgate-Palmolive-Peet, it was known, from the very beginning, simply as the Palmolive Building. The one in Manhattan, built when the company relocated to New York, is known as the Colgate-Palmolive Building.
2. Jane King Hession and Debra Pickrel, *Frank Lloyd Wright in New York: The Plaza Years, 1954–1959* (Gibbs Smith, 2007), 44.
3. Al Chase, "Plan Huge Palmolive Tower Across From Drake Hotel," *Chicago Tribune*, July 24, 1927, H1.
4. Henry J. B. Hoskins, "Structure and Equipment of the Palmolive Building," *Architectural Forum*, May 1930, pt. 1, p. 731.
5. "Tenants of New Building Hold Open House," *Chicago Tribune*, June 12, 1929, 12.
6. Henry J. B. Hoskins, "The Palmolive Building, Chicago," *Architectural Forum*, May 1930, 655.
7. Edward Alden Jewell, "A Torch to Light Us," *New York Times*, December 1, 1929.
8. Joseph J. Korom Jr., *The American Skyscraper, 1850–1940: A Celebration of Height* (Branden Books, 2008), 180.
9. John W. Stamper, *Chicago's North Michigan Avenue: Planning and Development, 1900–1930* (University of Chicago Press, 1991), 160–61.
10. "National Register of Historic Places Registration Form: Palmolive Building," 2003, National Park Service, United States Department of the Interior, 1.

11. "Today—All Day—the Palmolive Building is Open to the Inspection of All Chicago," *Chicago Tribune*, June 12, 1929, 12.
12. "Tenants of New Building Hold Open House," 12.
13. Clifford W. Spencer, "Practical Floodlighting," *Architectural Forum*, November 1930, 627. The earliest skyscraper to be illuminated was probably the Singer Building in New York City, which was floodlit in 1908, although the 1893 World's Columbian Exposition in Chicago was famous for its nocturnal splendor.
14. Mark J. Bouman, "'The Best Lighted City in the World': The Construction of a Nocturnal Landscape in Chicago," in *Chicago Architecture and Design, 1923–1993: Reconfiguration of an American Metropolis*, ed. John Zukowsky (Prestel, 1993), 40.
15. Thomas Leslie, *Chicago Skyscrapers, 1871–1934* (University of Illinois Press, 2013), 163.
16. "Tour d'Argent De Luxe Cafe for Boul Mich," *Chicago Tribune*, August 5, 1928, B1.
17. Raymond Wiggers, *Chicago in Stone and Clay: A Guide to the Windy City's Architectural Geology* (Northern Illinois University Press, 2022), 223.

EIGHT

1. Fred A. Chappell, "Little Journeys Through the Office of the Daily News," in *The Chicago Daily News Almanac and Year-Book for 1926*, ed. James Langland (Daily News Co., 1925), xviii.
2. Deborah Fulton Rau, "The Making of the Merchandise Mart: Air Rights and the Plan of Chicago, 1927–1931," in *Chicago Architecture and Design, 1923–1993: Reconfiguration of an American Metropolis*, ed. John Zukowsky (Prestel, 1993), 104.
3. Rau, "The Making of the Merchandise Mart," 104.
4. For a detailed contemporary analysis, see Anne Lee, "The Chicago Daily News Building," *Architectural Forum*, January 1930, pt. 1, pp. 21–48.
5. John V. Dodge, "'Air-Rights' and Locomotive Smoke," *American Builder*, August 1929, 60.
6. Lee, "Chicago Daily News Building," 22.
7. Greg Borzo, *Chicago's Fabulous Fountains* (Southern Illinois University Press, 2017), 137.
8. Teri J. Edelstein, "Chicago Encounters Art Deco," in *Art Deco Chicago*, ed. Robert Bruegmann (Chicago Art Deco Society, 2018), 38. On Brandt, see Joan Kahr, *Edgar Brandt: Master of Art Deco Ironwork* (Harry N. Abrams, 1999).
9. *Report of the New York City Landmarks Preservation Commission* (New York City Landmarks Preservation Commission, September 20, 2011), Designation List 448 LP-2425.
10. Eleanor Jewett, "Water Color Show is a Great Success," *Chicago Tribune*, May 9, 1926, F11.
11. Mary Lackritz Gray, *A Guide to Chicago's Murals* (University of Chicago Press, 2001), 360.
12. Blair Kamin, "A Hard Zell," *Chicago Tribune*, October 19, 2000; Dennis Rodkin and Sasha-Ann Simons, "What's That Building? Mural from the Old Daily News Building," WBEZ Chicago, April 21, 2026, https://www.wbez.org/architecture/2026/04/21/whats-that-building-mural-from-the-old-daily-news-building.

NINE

1. Robert C. Marsh, *150 Years of Opera in Chicago* (Northern Illinois University Press, 2006), 7–9.
2. "Our Mary, Hair Bobbed, Comes Home Sparkling," *Chicago Tribune*, October 22, 1921, 3.
3. Sergey Prokofiev, *Diaries: 1915–1923—Behind the Mask* (Cornell University Press, 2008), 656.
4. Edward Moore, "Romantic Dream of Opera to Be Realized Here Tomorrow Night," *Chicago Tribune*, November 3, 1929, H1.
5. "Chicago's Grand Opera," *Chicago Tribune*, November 3, 1929, 12.

6. Jay Pridmore and George A. Larson, *Chicago Architecture and Design* (Abrams, 2018), 124–25.
7. Sally A. Kitt Chappell, *Architecture and Planning of Graham, Anderson, Probst and White, 1912–1936* (University of Chicago Press, 1992), 15.
8. Chappell, *Architecture and Planning of Graham, Anderson, Probst and White*, 219.
9. Fred Eychaner and Betty Lou Weiss v. Theodore Gross and Roosevelt University, 747 N.E.2d 969 (2001).
10. "Commercial National Bank Building (Insull's Throne)," Chicagology, https://chicagology.com/skyscrapers/skyscrapers095/.
11. Carol Willis, "Light, Height, and Site: The Skyscraper in Chicago," in *Chicago Architecture and Design, 1923–1993: Reconfiguration of an American Metropolis*, ed. John Zukowsky (Prestel, 1993), 122.
12. Editorial, *Chicagoan*, November 23, 1929, 7.
13. John Ashenhurst and Ruth L. Ashenhurst, *All About Chicago* (Houghton Mifflin, 1933), 88.
14. James O'Donnell Bennett, "Throngs Hail Opera in Glory of New Home," *Chicago Tribune*, November 5, 1929, 1.
15. "Twenty-two Blanks," *Chicagoan*, February 25, 1929, 5.
16. Pauline A. Saliga, ed., *The Sky's the Limit: A Century of Chicago Skyscrapers* (Rizzoli, 1990), 153.
17. "Oral History of John Augur Holabird," interview by Susan S. Benjamin, Chicago Architects Oral History Project, The Ernest R. Graham Study Center for Architectural Drawings, Department of Architecture, Art Institute of Chicago, 1993, 33.
18. Herbert M. Johnson, "The Chicago Civic Opera and Its New Home," in *Chicago: The World's Youngest Great City*, ed. Rush C. Butler (American Publishers Corp, 1929), 70.
19. Chappell, *Architecture and Planning of Graham, Anderson, Probst and White*, 17.
20. Marsh, *150 Years of Opera in Chicago*, 102.
21. Robert Bruegmann, ed., *Art Deco Chicago* (Chicago Art Deco Society, 2018), 134.
22. Bruegmann, *Art Deco Chicago*, 17.
23. Mary Lackritz Gray, *A Guide to Chicago's Murals* (University of Chicago Press, 2001), 40.
24. Marsh, *150 Years of Opera in Chicago*, 108.

TEN

1. "Foreman Banks Pay $3,500,000 for Skyscraper," *Chicago Tribune*, June 17, 1925, 13.
2. H. F. Harrington, "News Item: After 'Time,'" *Chicagoan*, February 2, 1930, 11.
3. Raymond Wiggers, *Chicago in Stone and Clay: A Guide to the Windy City's Architectural Geology* (Northern Illinois University Press, 2022), 129. Geologist Wiggers explains that, technically, the stone is Mesoproterozoic Marcy Metanorthosite.
4. John Ashenhurst and Ruth L. Ashenhurst, *All About Chicago* (Houghton Mifflin, 1933), 52.
5. Laurie McGovern Petersen, ed., *AIA Guide to Chicago*, 4th ed. (University of Illinois Press, 2022), 84.
6. Walter Roth, "Demise of the Foreman-State Bank: Was It 'Shylock in Reverse'?," *Chicago Jewish History* 27, no. 3 (2003): 6–7, 10.

ELEVEN

1. For an illustration and explanation of the Michigan Avenue streetwall, see Commission on Chicago Landmarks, *Design Guidelines for the Historic Michigan Boulevard District* (Chicago Department of Planning and Development, 2016). Also see Blair Kamin, "Praise It or Raze It?," *Chicago Tribune*, February 27, 2002, B1.

2. John Ashenhurst and Ruth L. Ashenhurst, *All About Chicago* (Houghton Mifflin, 1933), 40.
3. Susan M. Baldwin and Jason D. Martin, "National Register of Historic Places Registration Form: Buckingham Building," 2000, National Park Service, United States Department of the Interior, sec. 7, p. 3.

TWELVE

1. Al Chase, "Plan $11,000,000 Tower on Site Costing $1.25 in 1837," *Chicago Tribune*, May 26, 1929, B1.
2. Pauline A. Saliga, ed., *The Sky's the Limit: A Century of Chicago's Skyscrapers* (Rizzoli, 1990), 155.
3. "Chicago's Century of Architectural Progress," *Chicago Tribune*, February 8, 1931, D1.
4. Mark J. Bouman, "'The Best Lighted City in the World': The Construction of a Nocturnal Landscape in Chicago," in *Chicago Architecture and Design, 1923–1993: Reconfiguration of an American Metropolis*, ed. John Zukowsky (Prestel, 1993), 43.
5. "New Sun Flash Beacon Shines as Colored Fan," *Chicago Tribune*, August 30, 1930, 2.
6. Advertisement, *Chicago Tribune*, October 8, 1929, 21.
7. "City's Fastest Elevators for New Skyscraper," *Chicago Tribune*, September 29, 1929, B7.
8. A. M. Nolan, "Chicagoans: A.N. Rebori," *Chicagoan*, August 31, 1929, 22.
9. A. N. Rebori, "A Lobby of Metal and Glass," *Architectural Forum*, November 1930, pt. 1, p. 638.
10. David McCracken, "5 Buildings You Shouldn't Overlook," *Chicago Tribune*, April 19, 1991, F30.
11. David Ibata, "Commercial Real Estate: 2 Edifices Due for Facelifts," *Chicago Tribune*, July 28, 1986, B3.

THIRTEEN

1. Guy Morton Briggs, *The Goal of the Builders: A Story of Trustees System Service* (Trustees System Publishing Corp., 1921), 30.
2. Benedict Dillion, "Two-O-One North Wells Street," *Greater Chicago Magazine*, November 1929, 6.
3. Edward Alden Jewell, "Art in Review," *New York Times*, January 31, 1933, 20.
4. "National Register of Historic Places Registration Form: Trustees System Service Building," 1998, National Park Service, United States Department of the Interior, 21.
5. Pauline A. Saliga, ed., *The Sky's the Limit: A Century of Chicago Skyscrapers* (Rizzoli, 1990), 163.
6. "Bankruptcy Receiver Named for Trustees System Service Corp.," *Chicago Tribune*, January 20, 1934, 23.
7. *Trustees System Service Building*, Landmark Designation Report (Chicago Department of Planning and Development, Landmarks Division, 2003), 2, 22.

FOURTEEN

1. Al Chase, "Forty-seven Story Tower to Replace Tacoma Building: World's First Skyscraper," *Chicago Tribune*, August 5, 1928, B1.
2. Raymond Wiggers, *Chicago in Stone and Clay: A Guide to the Windy City's Architectural Geology* (Northern Illinois University Press, 2022), 127.
3. Joseph J. Korom Jr., *The American Skyscraper, 1850–1940: A Celebration of Height* (Branden Books, 2008), 398.

4. Joseph M. Siry, *Air-Conditioning in Modern American Architecture, 1890–1970* (Pennsylvania State University Press, 2021).
5. Siry, *Air-Conditioning in Modern American Architecture*, 12–15.

FIFTEEN

1. Philip Hampson, "Chicago's Pit Will Rise 600 Feet Over City," *Chicago Tribune*, November 18, 1928, B1.
2. Museum of Science and Industry, *A Guide to 150 Years of Chicago Architecture* (Chicago Review Press, 1985), 57.
3. Editorial, *Chicagoan*, June 21, 1930, 7.
4. Editorial, *Chicagoan*, May 10, 1930, 3.
5. Edward Keegan, *The Chicago Board of Trade Building* (Pomegranate, 2005), 18.
6. Stuart Cohen, "The Chicago Tribune Tower Competition," *Chicago Art Deco Society Magazine*, Summer 2022, 12.
7. John Ashenhurst and Ruth L. Ashenhurst, *All About Chicago* (Houghton Mifflin, 1933), 60. "Volstead" refers to the federal Volstead Act of 1919, which enforced the Eighteenth Amendment banning the manufacture and sale of alcoholic beverages.
8. Charles Laurier, "Skyscrapers," in *The Encyclopedia of Chicago*, ed. James R. Grossman, Ann Durkin Keating, and Janice L. Reiff (University of Chicago Press, 2004), 26. See specifically the table titled "Chicago's Tallest Buildings since 1854."
9. Richard Guy Wilson, "Chicago Board of Trade Building," in *Art Deco Chicago*, ed. Robert Bruegmann (Chicago Art Deco Society, 2018), 162.
10. Raymond Wiggers, *Chicago in Stone and Clay: A Guide to the Windy City's Architectural Geology* (Northern Illinois University Press, 2022), 111.
11. Ralph J. Christian, "National Register of Historic Places Registration Form: Chicago Board of Trade Building," 1975, National Park Service, United States Department of the Interior, 1.
12. Wilson, "Chicago Board of Trade Building," 162.
13. Keegan, *Chicago Board of Trade Building*, 19.
14. Philip Hampson, "Ancient Goddess in Modern Form to Command City," *Chicago Tribune*, May 4, 1930, A14.
15. Oskar J. W. Hansen, "John Storrs—Sculptor," *Chicagoan*, January 14, 1928, 29.
16. Edmund McDevitt, "John Storrs, Ceres, and the Model Who Wasn't," *Art Can Save Us and Life's Ideas* (blog), January 18, 2019, https://www.edmcdevitt.org/john-storrs-ceres-and-the-model-who-wasnt/. According to her obituary in the *Chicago Tribune*, Madelyn Hammon FioRito Jones died in California in 2001 at age eighty-seven.
17. Richard Atwater, "Town Talk," *Chicagoan*, July 19, 1930, 15.
18. Quoted in Keegan, *Chicago Board of Trade Building*, 29–30.
19. Bryan Parks and J. M. Hansel, *Black Marbles of Northern Arkansas* (Arkansas Geological Survey, 1932), 6.
20. Richard Atwater, "Town Talk," *Chicagoan*, May 10, 1930, 15–16.
21. Ashenhurst and Ashenhurst, *All About Chicago*, 59.
22. Louis Pomerantz, "Treatment and Mounting of 'Ceres,' a Large Mural Painting on Fabric by John Norton," *Journal of the American Institute for Conservation* 24, no. 1 (1984): 14–22.

SIXTEEN

1. Rima Lunin Schultz and Ellen Skerrett, "Sister Builders in Chicago," University of Notre Dame Cushwa Center, American Catholic Studies Newsletter, Spring 2015,

https://cushwa.nd.edu/publications/american-catholic-studies-newsletter/spring-2015-newsletter/sister-builders-in-chicago/.

2. *Mundelein College Skyscraper Building*, Landmark Designation Report (City of Chicago, 2006).
3. Pauline Margaret Abraham Tarvardian, "An Uncompromising Commitment to Mission: Mundelein College and the Advancement of Women's Higher Education 1930–1950" (PhD diss., Loyola University Chicago, 1990), 39–40.
4. Tarvardian, "An Uncompromising Commitment to Mission," 55–58.
5. Laurie McGovern Petersen, ed., *AIA Guide to Chicago*, 4th ed. (University of Illinois Press, 2022), 441.
6. "The Mundelein College Skyscraper," Loyola University Chicago Women and Leadership Archives, https://www.luc.edu/wla/mundeleincollegebuildings/themundeleincollegeskyscraper/.
7. James O'Donnell Bennett, "Pope Praises Great Catholic College Here," *Chicago Tribune*, September 27, 1931, 1.
8. Tarvardian, "An Uncompromising Commitment to Mission," 101.
9. Bennett, "Pope Praises Great Catholic College Here," 1.
10. Tarvardian, "An Uncompromising Commitment to Mission," 102.
11. Quoted in Tarvardian, "An Uncompromising Commitment to Mission," 94.
12. Raymond Wiggers, *Chicago in Stone and Clay: A Guide to the Windy City's Architectural Geology* (Northern Illinois University Press, 2022), 286.

SEVENTEEN

1. Frank F. Sengstock, "The Largest Building in the World," *Western Architect*, December 1930, 205. Some tall buildings in Chicago were built on lots even smaller than standard ones. The 519-foot-high Mather Tower (1928), for example, is on a 100-by-65-foot lot, which accounts for its rocket-like profile.
2. Jay Pridmore, *The Merchandise Mart* (Pomegranate, 2003), 13.
3. Deborah Fulton Rau, "The Making of the Merchandise Mart: Air Rights and the Plan of Chicago, 1927–1931," in *Chicago Architecture and Design, 1923–1993: Reconfiguration of an American Metropolis*, ed. John Zukowsky (Prestel, 1993), 102.
4. Thomas Leslie, *Chicago Skyscrapers, 1871–1934* (University of Illinois Press, 2013), 171.
5. Sengstock, "The Largest Building in the World," 206.
6. Pridmore, *The Merchandise Mart*, 12.
7. Jean L. Guarino, "Merchandise Mart," in *Art Deco Chicago*, ed. Robert Bruegmann (Chicago Art Deco Society, 2018), 179.
8. Rau, "The Making of the Merchandise Mart," 112.
9. David Roeder, "Mart's Makeover," *Chicago Sun-Times*, May 29, 2023, 4.
10. Christopher Borrelli, "The Swab Squad: 3 Women, Armed with Makeshift Q-Tips, Bring Merchandise Mart Lobby Murals Back to Life," *Chicago Tribune*, July 16, 2014, D1.

EIGHTEEN

1. "Y.M.C.A. Plans to Oust Gangs with Athletics," *Chicago Tribune*, January 25, 1930, 11.
2. Emmett Dedmon, *Great Enterprises: 100 Years of the YMCA of Metropolitan Chicago* (Rand McNally, 1957), 242.
3. Dedmon, *Great Enterprises*, 242.
4. "Two Blasts Jar Near North Side," *Chicago Tribune*, February 9, 1930, 16.
5. "$2,750,000 'Y' Ready to Open Next Sunday," *Chicago Tribune*, October 25, 1931, D4.
6. For a detailed and informed description, see Susan Baldwin Burian, "National Register

of Historic Places Registration Form: Victor F. Lawson House YMCA," June 2016, National Park Service, United States Department of the Interior.

NINETEEN

1. *Old Chicago Main Post Office Building*, Landmark Designation Report (Chicago Department of Planning and Development, Landmarks Division, 2017), 12.
2. "Says New Post Office Will Be Big Money Saver," *Chicago Tribune*, July 12, 1931, A11; "New Post Office Dedicated; To Save Millions," *Chicago Tribune*, February 16, 1933, 7.
3. "Way is Cleared for $14,000,000 Chicago P.O.," *Chicago Tribune*, October 16, 1930, 1.
4. "Building of Post Office to Give Work to 6,000," *Chicago Tribune*, October 17, 1930, 4.
5. Sally A. Kitt Chappell, *Architecture and Planning of Graham, Anderson, Probst and White, 1912–1936: Transforming Tradition* (University of Chicago Press, 1992), 250–51.
6. "New P.O. Has World's Biggest Welded Pipe Job," *Chicago Tribune*, February 19, 1933, 17.
7. "Plan Airport on Top of Chicago's New Postoffice," *Chicago Tribune*, July 21, 1927, 7.
8. *Old Chicago Main Post Office Building*, 19.
9. Chappell, *Architecture and Planning of Graham, Anderson, Probst and White*, 250.
10. Blair Kamin, "Post Office Plan Fails to Deliver First-Class Design," *Chicago Tribune*, July 24, 2011, 15.
11. David Roeder, "Few Winners, Many Losers as Office Building Debt and Vacancy Worsens," *Chicago Sun-Times*, July 24, 2023, 4.

TWENTY

1. Quoted in Robert Goldsborough, "City of Deco," *Chicago Tribune*, June 1, 1997, SM12.
2. Al Chase, "Jobs for 7,500 as Fuller Gets Field's Contract," *Chicago Tribune*, July 18, 1931, 5.
3. Stephen Becker, *Marshall Field III: A Biography* (Simon & Schuster, 1964), 117, 127.
4. "Oral History of Charles F. Murphy," Chicago Architects Oral History Project, The Ernest R. Graham Study Center for Architectural Drawings, Department of Architecture, Art Institute of Chicago, 1995, 20.
5. "Start Wrecking Old Insurance Building Today," *Chicago Tribune*, September 26, 1931, 22.
6. "Was the Home Insurance Building in Chicago the First Skyscraper of Skeleton Construction?," *Architectural Record*, August 1934, 118.
7. "Mr. Waid Corrects Us," *Pencil Points* 10, no. 9 (1929): 642.
8. "Tenants Enter First Unit of Field Building," *Chicago Tribune*, May 29, 1932, 10.
9. Joseph J. Korom Jr., *The American Skyscraper 1850–1940: A Celebration of Height* (Branden Books, 2008), 448.
10. Thomas Leslie, *Chicago Skyscrapers, 1871–1934* (University of Illinois Press, 2013), 172.
11. Raymond Wiggers, *Chicago in Stone and Clay: A Guide to the Windy City's Architectural Geology* (Northern Illinois University Press, 2022), 113–15.
12. Korom, *American Skyscraper*, 449.
13. "The Field Building, Chicago's Newest Skyscraper," *Architectural Record*, August 1934, 120.
14. "Field Building to Have an Air Cooling System," *Chicago Tribune*, April 9, 1932, 27.
15. Eleanor Page, "Lunch Clubs for the Young Man on His Way Up," *Chicago Tribune*, June 24, 1962, C6; Jean L. Guarino, "Field Building," in *Art Deco Chicago*, ed. Robert Bruegmann (Chicago Art Deco Society, 2018), 233.

CONCLUSION

1. For a comprehensive and illustrated contemporary view of many aspects of the fair, see "A Century of Progress: Chicago Exposition of 1933," *Architectural Record*, May 1933, 342–74. For a list of the major buildings and their architects, see Lisa D. Schrenk, *Building a Century of Progress: The Architecture of Chicago's 1933–34 World's Fair* (University of Minnesota Press, 2007), 265–67.
2. Jack Hartray, "Purgatory and Paradise," in *Chicago Architecture: Holabird and Root 1880–1992*, ed. Werner Blaser (Birkhäuser Verlag, 1992), 13. Walter Gropius (1883–1969) was the founder of the famous German art school the Bauhaus and a leading figure in twentieth-century modernist architecture.
3. Neil Harris, "Decomania, the Paths to an Enthusiasm," in *Art Deco Chicago*, ed. Robert Bruegmann (Chicago Art Deco Society, 2018), 70.

INDEX

A

adaptive reuse, 151
Addams, Jane, 57. *See also* Jane Addams Homes
Adler, Dankmar, 120
Adler, David, 172
Adler Planetarium, 15
agriculture, 125–26
AIA Guide to Chicago, 37, 91
air rights, 68, 146
air-conditioning, 119–21, 157, 169
Alcoa aluminum, 127
Alférez, Enrique, 64
Allegheny metal, 104
Allesandro, Paul, 31
American Automobile Association (AAA), 29
American National Bank and Trust Company, 93
American Society of Heating, Refrigerating, and Air-Conditioning, 121
antisemitism, 23
apartments, 46, 51, 157. *See also* cooperative apartments (co-ops)
Architectural Forum, 47, 60, 62, 69, 82–83, 104
Architectural Record, 6, 9, 18, 20, 46, 169
Areologist Publishing Company, 121
Armour Building, 174
Armour Institute of Technology, 103
Art Deco: color in, 11–13, 48, 55–57; cultural influences of, 6–7, 47, 49–50; design, 13, 20, 79; history of, 2–5; murals, 30, 83, 97–98, 128–29, 148, 151; ornamentation, 5, 11–13, 30–31, 69, 82. *See also* avant-garde style; moderne; motifs
Art Institute of Chicago, 132
Attic Club, 172. *See also* Field Building
Auditorium Theatre, 78–79, 80

automobile clubs, 28
automobiles, 4, 15, 28–29
avant-garde style, 2, 5, 24. *See also* Art Deco; moderne

B

Baird & Warner, 46
Bakelite, 4, 174
bas-reliefs, 11, 21, 64, 69, 107, 126
Bauhaus, 2
Beaux-Arts style, 7, 18, 71, 78, 85, 117, 159
Beersman, Charles, 15, 90
Bergman, Ruth G., 47
biocalcarenite, 11. *See also* Indiana limestone; limestone
Bosley Wrecking Company, 90
Boyd, John Taylor, Jr., 9
Boyington, W. W., 125, 127
Brâncusi, Constantin, 127
Brandt, Edgar, 69–70
Brasco Manufacturing Company of Chicago, 13
brass, 43, 69, 129, 169
bronze, 13, 20–21, 43, 57, 69, 83, 119, 148, 164, 169
Brown, Frank Elam, 15. *See also* Chicago Daily News Building; Chicago Motor Club; 333 North Michigan
Brown, Walter F., 160
Buckingham Building, 10, 15, 95; materials, 96, 98–99; motifs, 96–98
Burnham, Daniel, 78, 103, 137, 144
Burnham, Daniel, Jr., 53
Burnham Brothers, 53, 173
Burns, John J., 117. *See also* One North La Salle

C

caissons, 10, 62, 68, 108, 146, 154. *See also* Smith, William Sooy
campaniles, 55–57. *See also* pinnacles
Carbide and Carbon Building, 53; materials, 56–57; motifs, 57; myths, 55–56; restoration of, 35, 57
cast iron, 20, 30, 61, 156
Central Life Insurance Building, 53
Central Post Office, 6, 159; development of, 160–62; ornamentation, 164–65
Chamber of Commerce Building, 88, 90
chandeliers, 83
Chassaing, Edouard, 35
Chatten, Melville C., 41. *See also* Perkins, Chatten & Hammond
Chicago: aesthetics of, 11–13; architecture firms, 14–15, 18–19, 21, 95 (*see also* Graham, Anderson, Probst & White (GAPW); Holabird & Root); arts and culture in, 77–78, 97–98, 104, 147; banks, 41–43, 117–18; buildings of, 117; Catholicism in, 137; colleges of, 99, 135–36 (*see also* Loyola University; Mundelein Center); geography of, 39, 41, 46–47, 61, 68, 126; industry, 35–36, 41, 78, 87, 125, 147, 154, 160; Midway Gardens, 5–6, 49; Motor Row, 28–29; murals, 30, 83, 97–98, 128–29, 148, 151; neighborhoods, 35, 46, 60, 148; population, 41; real

estate, 31, 46–47, 113, 168, 171; setback ordinance, 6–7; skyscrapers, 6–7, 14–15, 168; South Loop, 98–99; transportation in, 61, 78, 162–64
Chicago and North Western Railway, 69, 146
Chicago Architecture Center, 176
Chicago Art Deco Society, 4, 31, 55, 176
Chicago Beach Hotel, 47
Chicago Board of Trade Building, 10, 123; design of, 126; motifs, 129; ornamentation, 127–29; restoration of, 132; statues, 132
Chicago Century of Progress Exposition, 104, 156, 160, 173
Chicago Club, 95
Chicago Daily News, 67–68, 70–71, 75
Chicago Daily News Building, 15, 67; air rights of, 68; design of, 69; mural, 70–73; ornamentation, 69
Chicago Grand Opera Company, 77, 85
Chicago Motor Club, 10, 27, 57; commission of, 27–28; materials, 30–31; motifs, 30; renovation of, 31
Chicago Opera Association, 77
Chicago Plan Commission, 15, 144, 155, 159, 165. *See also* Simpson, James; Wacker, Charles H.
Chicago Public Library, 160
Chicago School, 104, 174. *See also* Art Deco
Chicago Sun-Times Building, 75
Chicago Temple Building, 61
Chicago Theatre, 35
Chicago Tribune, 5, 7–8, 20, 23, 37–38, 60–62
Chicago Union Terminal Company, 160
Chicago Zoning Commission, 46
Chicagoan, 18, 23–24, 46–47, 79–80, 90, 123, 128–29, 144
Circassian walnut, 63
Civic Opera House, 35, 77; design of, 78–80; materials, 78–82; ornamentation, 82–83; ownership of, 85; restoration of, 85. *See also* Lyric Opera House
Civic Theater, 78
Clarence F. Buckingham Memorial Fountain, 96
Clark Street Bridge, 15
Cobb, Henry Ives, 159
Coffey, Justitia, 137
Colgate-Palmolive-Peet Company, 59
Collins, Charles, 23. *See also* Tavern Club
Commission on Chicago Landmarks, 30–31, 39, 119, 132
cooperative apartments (co-ops), 46–47. *See also* apartments
Corbett, Henry Wiley, 11
Corcoran, John Charles, 107–8, 113. *See also* Trustees System Service Building
Coughlin, John "Bathhouse," 79
Coyote Building, 43. *See also* Northwest Tower
cubism, 24, 127
cupolas, 20, 43
Curry, John Steuart, 23
curtain walls, 35
Curtis Lighting Company, 62
Cutten, Arthur, 132

D

D. H. Burnham and Co., 53, 126, 168
Daley, Richard M., 69
Davies, Bill, 164–65
DeGolyer, Robert, 48, 51
DePaul Art Museum, 23
D'Esposito, Joshua, 68, 160
du Pont, Henry F., 47
DuSable Bridge, 17

E

E. F. Wilson & Co., 41
École des Beaux-Arts, 103. *See also* Beaux-Arts style
Edison, Thomas, 78
1893 World's Columbian Exposition, 7, 47
elevators: Buckingham Building, 99; Carbide and Carbon Building, 56–57; Chicago Board of Trade Building, 128–29; Chicago Daily News Building, 69; Chicago Motor Club, 31; Field Building, 169; Foreman State National Bank, 91; innovations in, 9, 43, 51, 102–3, 171; La Salle-Wacker Building, 104; Mundelein Center, 137–38, 141; Northwest Tower, 42–43; One North La Salle, 119–20; Palmolive Building, 62, 64–65; Powhatan Apartments, 46, 51; 333 North Michigan, 20
Exposition Internationale des Arts Décoratifs et Industriels Modernes (1925), 2–7, 35, 127. *See also* Art Deco

F

Fairman, Margaret T., 49
Fannie May, 21
Farwell, Field, and Company, 144
Field, Marshall, 144, 167
Field, Marshall, III, 168–69, 172
Field Building, 10, 14, 144, 167; construction of, 168–69; occupants of, 171–72; ornamentation, 169. *See also* Attic Club
Field Enterprises, 75
Field Museum, 144, 168
Fisher, Charles, 140
Fisher, Nairne W., 137
floodlights, 62
Foreman, Gerhard, 91
Foreman, Oscar G., 88, 91
Foreman State National Bank, 87; closure of, 91–93; design of, 90; materials, 91; motifs, 90
Formica, 4
Fujikawa Johnson and Associates, 132

G

Gage and Haines, 125
Galena and Union Railroad, 125
Garard, Elzy Anderson, 47

Garden, Mary, 77–78
General Bronze Corporation, 13
Glickman, John, 79
Goettsch Partners, 21
Gold Coast, 46, 60, 117
Goodhue, Bertram, 11, 125–26
Gothic style, 7
Graham, Anderson, Probst & White (GAPW): Armour Building, 174; Central Post Office, 160–62; Civic Opera House, 78; creation of, 14–15; Field Building, 167–68; Foreman State National Bank, 90; Merchandise Mart, 78, 144–46. *See also* Graham, Ernest
Graham, Ernest, 78, 168. *See also* Graham, Anderson, Probst & White (GAPW)
"Grand Art Deco formula," 11, 37, 41–42, 164. *See also* Wiggers, Raymond
granite: black, 55–56, 164, 169; Charcoal Black, 117; Cold Stone Pearl Pink, 126; Lake Placid Blue, 90
Grant Park, 96
Great Chicago Fire of 1871, 40–42, 77, 91, 144
Great Depression, 42, 62, 85, 91, 174
Great Recession of 2008, 31, 43, 75
Grenman, Bertell, 7
gridiron, 82
Grupo Habita, 43
Guérin, Jules, 83, 85, 148, 151
Gunderson, Magnus, 15. *See also* Merchandise Mart

H

Hammond, C. Herrick, 41. *See also* Perkins, Chatten & Hammond
Harboe Architects, 132
Hard Rock International, 57
hardpan, 10. *See also* caissons
Harrington & King Perforating Company, 13
Hartshorne Plunkard Architecture, 31
Head, Walter W., 93
Hermant, Leon, 118–19
Hillier, Bevis, 3–4
Holabird, John Augur, 5, 14, 18, 63. *See also* Holabird & Root
Holabird, John Augur, Jr., 2, 5, 11, 82
Holabird & Roche, 18. *See also* Holabird & Root
Holabird & Root, 14, 37; Buckingham Building, 96; Chicago Board of Trade Building, 125–26, 129; Chicago Daily News Building, 67, 69; Chicago Motor Club, 33; Chrysler Motors Building, 173; creation of, 18; La Salle-Wacker Building, 103; Palmolive Building, 59, 63, 65; projects of, 13, 23, 173; 333 North Michigan, 18, 20–21
Home Insurance Building, 168
Hoover, Herbert, 65
Hughes, Charles Evans, 47
Hyde Park, 6, 47

I

Illinois and Michigan Canal, 125
impressionism, 48

Indiana limestone, 41–43, 69, 90, 102, 117, 126, 140, 162, 169
insulae, 45
Insull, Samuel, 78–79, 85
Insurance Center, 36
International Museum of Surgical Science, 36
iron, 69, 113

J

Jahn, Helmut, 132
Jane Addams Homes, 23. *See also* Addams, Jane
Janszen, John T., 121
Jazz Age, 3, 14, 28, 61, 91
Jenney, William Le Baron, 15, 120, 168
journalism, 67–69
Julia C. Lathrop Homes, 51

K

Kane, Isabella, 136
Karbowski, Krzysztof, 43
Kennedy, Joseph, 148

L

La Salle, René-Robert Cavelier, Sieur de, 118
La Salle-Wacker Building, 10, 101; beacon, 102; design of, 102–3; elements of, 102; elevators in, 103; materials, 103; renovation of, 103
La Salle-Wacker Building Corporation, 101
Lake Shore Trust and Savings Bank, 65
landmarks, 57
Landmarks Illinois, 31, 71
Langerbeck, Mary Therese, 139
Laramie State Bank, 35
Lawson, Victor F., 69, 154
Lawson House YMCA, 153; development of, 155–56; ornamentation, 156; restoration of, 156–57
Leiter, Levi, 144
Lewis, Samuel R., 121
lighting: beacons, 13, 64–65; electric, 125; floodlights, 43, 62, 102, 169
limestone: Indiana, 41–43, 61, 69, 90, 102, 117, 126, 140, 162, 169; Morton gneiss, 20; Salem, 11
Loyola University, 23, 104, 137–38, 141
Lux, Eugene Van Breeman, 109, 111
Lux, Gwen, 109, 111
Lyric Opera, 85
Lyric Opera House, 85. *See also* Civic Opera House

M

Magnificent Mile, 17
marble: Alabama madre cream, 129; Batesville, 129; Belgian Black, 57; Bottocino, 69; Colorado Yule, 169; green, 91; Notre Dame, 63, 99; Numidian, 113; Paitone Breccia, 169; Tav-

ernelle, 129; Tennessee, 57, 63, 113; Tennessee champion pink, 129; travertine, 57, 113; verde antico, 20, 113; Vermont, 21
Marc Merckx Interiors, 43
Marshall Field & Co., 70, 144
mass media, 67
McCarthy, Joseph W., 137
McClurg, Verne O., 15. *See also* Buckingham Building; Chicago Board of Trade Building
McGraw-Hill Building, 108, 111
McKnight, Joseph, 121
Meiere, Hildreth, 11
Merchandise Mart, 6, 102, 143, 162, 167; development of, 144–47; ornamentation, 148–51
Methodist Book Concern, 10
Meyer, Alvin W., 69, 126–28
Michigan Avenue, 17–18, 21, 23–24, 28, 37, 53, 60, 95–96
Michigan Avenue Bridge, 53. *See also* DuSable Bridge
Mies van der Rohe, Ludwig, 51, 59, 174
Miesian, 174. *See also* Mies van der Rohe, Ludwig
Miller, Edgar, 23, 104, 111–13, 174
Milwaukee cream brick, 96
moderne, 2–5, 9, 23–24, 90, 137, 155, 160, 174. *See also* Art Deco; avant-garde style
modernism, 7
modernity, 2
Monadnock Building, 10
Monel metal, 13, 104
Morgan, Charles L., 48–49
Mosaic Overmantels, 48
motifs: birds, 31, 51, 90, 119; botanical, 31, 90, 96, 127, 129, 140; chevron, 91, 99, 119, 143, 148, 156; geometric, 30, 31, 57, 71, 85, 90, 118, 127, 140, 164; industry, 111–13; Native American, 30, 48, 127, 148; nature, 31; papyrus, 61; "speed lines," 141; transportation, 99, 118, 148; vegetal, 90; wheat, 127; zigzag, 71, 140. *See also* Art Deco
Motley, Archibald, Jr., 23
Motor Row, 28–29
Mundelein, George, 136–37
Mundelein Center, 6, 135; construction of, 136–37; design of, 137–40
Mundelein pendulum, 138–39
Mundie, William Bryce, 120–21
Murphy, Charles F., 168
Murphy, John T., 31
Musée des Art Décoratifs, 3
Museum of Modern Art, 174
Museum of Science and Industry, 15

N

National Association of Real Estate Boards, 95
National Register of Historic Places, 35, 99, 139
National Terra Cotta Company, 13
Neoclassical style, 7
1933–1934 Century of Progress Exposition, 104, 156, 160, 173–75
Noel, Joseph R., 41
Noonan, Clifford, 14, 78

North Shore Stone Company, 140
Northwest Tower, 39; construction of, 10, 41–42; materials, 43; renovation of, 43
Northwestern Terra Cotta Co., 35
Northwestern University, 9, 154
Norton, John Warner, 23–24, 30–31, 70–71, 131–32

O

"ocean liner style," 5–6, 20
One North La Salle, 10, 13, 69, 115; air-conditioning in, 120–21; design of, 118; history of, 121

P

Palmer, Potter, 144
Palmolive Building, 59, 102; beacon, 62, 65; design of, 60–62; materials, 60–62, 63; remodel of, 64
parapets, 37, 48
Peck, Philip F. W., 101
Perkins, Chatten & Hammond, 41–43. *See also* Lawson House YMCA; Northwest Tower
Perkins, Dwight H., 41. *See also* Perkins, Chatten & Hammond
Picasso, Pablo, 127
pinnacles, 55–56, 102. *See also* campaniles
Playboy Corporation, 64
Pomerantz, Louis, 132
postmodernism, 3
Powhatan Apartments, 45; design of, 47–48; motifs, 49–51
preservation, 3, 31, 57, 132, 157. *See also* renovation; restoration
Prohibition, 21, 30
Prokofiev, Sergei, 78
Pullman Cars, style of, 35
pyramidal roofs, 79, 125, 126–27, 146

R

railroads, 4, 68–69, 78–79, 95, 125, 144–46, 160
Ramsey, Afton C., 121
Randall, Frank A., 15. *See also* Lawson House YMCA
Randolph Tower, 35
Rebori, Andrew Nicholas, 103; death of, 104; designs of, 104, 173, 174
Rebori, Wentworth, Dewey & McCormick, 103
Regent Room, 121
Reiss, Winold, 23
Reliance Building, 35, 82
Rena Hartman, Inc., 20
renovation, 21, 113, 132, 141, 147–48. *See also* preservation; restoration
restoration, 50, 57, 85, 143, 151. *See also* preservation; renovation
Roche, Martin, 18
Rockefeller, Percy, 47
Rodman & Linn, 99
Root, Elihu, 47

Root, John W., 2, 14, 21, 63. *See also* Holabird & Root
Royal College of Building Technology, 117

S

Saarinen, Eero, 111
Saarinen, Eliel, 7, 20
salamanders, 68
Sandburg, Carl, 24, 68
Savoy-Plaza Hotel, 36
Schmidt, Jean Dolores Bertha, 137
Schuybroek, Nicolas, 43
sculpture, 11, 21, 35, 69, 109, 111, 118–19, 127–29, 132, 140, 156
Sears, Roebuck and Co., 148, 160
Seminary of the Sacred Heart, 135
setback ordinance, 61, 108, 126, 139
Shaw, Alfred, 15, 78, 144, 168. *See also* Civic Opera House; Field Building; Merchandise Mart
Shedd, John G., 47
Simpson, James, 15, 144. *See also* Chicago Plan Commission
Sisters of Charity of the Blessed Virgin Mary (BVMs), 135–37
skyscrapers, 95; design of, 13–14, 42, 148, 158; history of, 14–15, 168, 172–74; inspiration for, 6–7; materials for, 11, 90, 169; tenancy of, 20–21, 37, 43, 62, 95; verticality of, 11, 27, 48, 57. *See also specific buildings*
Smith, Alfred E., 103
Smith, William Sooy, 10. *See also* caissons
spandrels, 43, 48, 61, 91, 96
Sperry, Elmer G., 65
Sperry Gyroscope Company, 65
spires, 11, 48. *See also* cupolas
St. Jane Hotel, 57
stainless steel, 104
Starrett, William A., 9–11, 15, 35
State Bank of Chicago, 91
steel, 9–13, 65, 68, 82, 99, 104–5, 144–46, 160
Steif, Benjamin Leo, 33, 36–37
Sterling Bronze Company, 83
Stewart, Albert, 20
Stone, Edward Durell, 111
Storrs, John, 127–29
Strong, Walter A., 67
Sullivan, Louis, 11, 90, 120
Sun Flash, 102. *See also* La Salle-Wacker Building

T

Tacoma Building, 115, 168
Taft, Lorado, 21, 64
Taussig, Meredith, 119
Tavern Club, 21–24
television, 71

10 West Elm: design of, 36–37; materials, 33–35
terra-cotta, 33–36, 55, 91
terrazzo, 11, 20, 31, 43, 69, 104, 143, 169
333 North Michigan, 10, 14, 65; design of, 7, 17–20; materials, 20–21; murals, 23–24; ornamentation, 21–24
torchieres, 83
Traylor, Melvin A., 93
Tribune Tower, 7, 17, 42
TripTik, 30
Trustees System Service Building, 15, 107; construction of, 108; deconversion of, 113; design of, 109–11
Tudor Gothic style, 36

V

Vanderbilt, Alva, 47
Victor F. Lawson Memorial Fountain, 69
Vitrolite, 4
Vitzthum, Karl M., 117
Vitzthum and Burns, 117

W

Wabash Arts Corridor, 98
Wacker, Charles H., 159. *See also* Chicago Plan Commission; La Salle-Wacker Building
Waid, D. Everett, 168
Wallace, Dwight G., 7
Warren, Clinton J., 46
Water Tower, 125
Weisberg, Julius "Dollie," 121
Welsh, William P., 23
Westinghouse Electric Elevator Company, 43
Whiston Group, 57
White, Charles E., Jr., 34
White, Howard, 168
Wicker Park District, 39, 43
Wiener Secession, 5
Wiggers, Raymond, 11, 20, 118, 126. *See also* "Grand Art Deco formula"
WMAQ (radio station), 69
World War I, 2
World War II, 57, 148, 156, 174–76
World's Fair, 104, 118, 173
Wright, Frank Lloyd, 5, 35, 48–49, 59
Wrigley Building, 15, 35, 62, 108
wrought-iron, 46, 70, 146

Z

Zell, Sam, 71, 75